Productivity versus OSHA and EPA Regulations

Research for Business Decisions, No. 86

Richard N. Farmer, Series Editor

Professor of International Business
Indiana University

Other Titles in This Series

No. 76	*Management in Post-Mao China: An Insider's View*	Joseph Y. Battat
No. 82	*Accounting in Developing Countries: A Framework for Standard Setting*	Felix E. Amenkhienan
No. 83	*The Flaw in Japanese Management*	Haruo Takagi
No. 84	*The Impact of Cybernation Technology on Black Automotive Workers in the U.S.*	Samuel D. K. James
No. 85	*Innovative Reporting in Foreign Currency Translation*	Denise M. Guithues
No. 87	*The Exporting Behavior of Manufacturing Firms*	Somkid Jatusripitak
No. 88	*The Impact on Consumers of a Restructured Personal Federal Tax*	John Huss Green
No. 89	*Managing the Medical Enterprise: A Study of Physician Managers*	Carol Betson

Productivity versus OSHA and EPA Regulations

by
Wayne B. Gray

UMI RESEARCH PRESS
Ann Arbor, Michigan

ROBERT MANNING
STROZIER LIBRARY

Soc
HC
110
I52
G73
1986

MAY 22 1986

Tallahassee, Florida

Copyright © 1986, 1984
Wayne Burger Gray
All rights reserved

Produced and distributed by
UMI Research Press
an imprint of
University Microfilms International
A Xerox Information Resources Company
Ann Arbor, Michigan 48106

Library of Congress Cataloging in Publication Data

Gray, Wayne B. (Wayne Burger), 1955-
Productivity versus OSHA and EPA regulations.

(Research for business decisions ; no. 86)
Revision of thesis (Ph.D.)—Harvard University, 1984.
  Bibliography: p.
  Includes index.
  1. Industrial productivity—United States. 2. United States—Manufactures. 3. Factory and trade waste—Law and legislation—United States—Compliance costs.
4. Industrial safety—Law and legislation—United States—Compliance costs. I. Title. II. Series.
HC110.I52G73 1986   338'.06'0973   85-28873
ISBN 0-8357-1721-6 (alk. paper)

To my parents,
who never stopped encouraging me

Contents

List of Figures   *ix*

List of Tables   *xi*

Acknowledgments   *xiii*

1   Introduction   *1*

2   Productivity   *3*
     2.1   Introduction
     2.2   Productivity Models
     2.3   Measurement Techniques
     2.4   Problems with Growth Accounting
     2.5   Single Factor Productivity Measures
     2.6   Conclusion

3   OSHA and EPA Regulation   *13*
     3.1   Introduction
     3.2   Environmental Pollution
     3.3   Worker Safety and Health
     3.4   Summary

4   Regulation's Impact on Productivity   *37*
     4.1   Introduction
     4.2   Impact on Firms' Behavior
     4.3   Impact on Productivity
     4.4   Modeling the Impact
     4.5   Conclusion

viii Contents

5 Productivity Slowdown: Evidence and Explanations *45*
    5.1 Introduction
    5.2 Evidence for Slowdown
    5.3 Possible Explanations for the Slowdown
    5.4 Previous Studies
    5.5 Summary

6 Data Description *55*
    6.1 Introduction
    6.2 Productivity Data
    6.3 Regulation Measures: Compliance Costs
    6.4 Regulation Measures: Enforcement
    6.5 Other Data Sets
    6.6 Summary

7 Regulation's Impact on Productivity: Empirical Analysis *67*
    7.1 Introduction
    7.2 Productivity Slowdown
    7.3 Simple Regulation: Productivity Relationship
    7.4 Possible Objections
    7.5 Extensions and Tests
    7.6 Panel Data Analysis
    7.7 Long-Run Relationship
    7.8 Conclusions

8 Benefits from Regulation *91*
    8.1 Introduction
    8.2 Previous Estimates
    8.3 Targeting
    8.4 Benefits
    8.5 Conclusions

9 Conclusions and Future Work *97*

Appendix: Distribution of Regulation Data *101*

Notes *103*

Bibliography *109*

Index *115*

List of Figures

3.1. Individual and Aggregate Benefits and Costs from Pollution Cleanup *15*

3.2. Costs of Missing the Optimum: Price vs. Quantity Parameters *19*

3.3. Wage Differentials due to Job Hazards *27*

5.1. Sectoral Labor Productivity, 1951–80 *46*

5.2. Sectoral Multifactor Productivity, 1951–80 *50*

7.1. Weighted Industry Productivity, 1961–80 *69*

List of Tables

5.1. Labor Productivity Growth Rates   47

5.2. Multifactor Productivity Growth Rates   48

6.1. Major Data Sources   56

7.1. Average Industry Productivity Growth Rates   70

7.2. Descriptive Statistics   71

7.3. Initial Regression Results   72

7.4. Outlier and Non-Linearity Analysis   75

7.5. Non-Parametric Analysis   76

7.6. Energy Intensity and Capital Intensity   78

7.7. Cyclical and Declining Industry Controls   79

7.8. Analysis Including R&D Data   80

7.9. Impact of Weighted Regulation Measures   82

7.10. Other Impacts of Regulation   84

7.11. Cross-Industry "Production Function" Models   85

7.12. Panel Data Analysis   88

7.13. Long-Run Impact of Regulation   *90*

8.1. Targeting of Enforcement Effort   *94*

8.2. Benefits from OSHA Safety Inspections   *95*

A.1. Regulation Measures: Top 10 Industries and Distributions   *102*

Acknowledgments

This work would not have been possible without the support and encouragement of many individuals and institutions. I am indebted to the Sloan Foundation and the National Bureau of Economic Research for financial support; the Occupational Safety and Health Administration, the Environmental Protection Agency, and other government agencies for making data available; and the National Bureau of Economic Research, again, for providing a pleasant and supportive research environment.

Many individuals made helpful comments and suggestions, including David Ellwood, Hendrick Houthakker, Casey Ichniowski, Frank Lichtenberg, and Olivia Mitchell. Carol Jones provided many useful comments on an early draft. I also benefitted from comments received when I presented this research at the Harvard labor seminar, at the bureau's Summer Institute, and at the campuses of several prospective employers during the winter of 1984. I am particularly grateful to my advisers, Richard Freeman and Zvi Griliches, for their support and suggestions over the long haul. Any errors and omissions are my own responsibility.

Finally, I would like to thank my wife, Liz, for putting up with many late nights over the last few years. She also drew the figures, keypunched some of the data, and provided constant encouragement. I might have managed to finish this without her help, but I'm certainly glad I didn't have to.

1

Introduction

The slowdown in productivity growth in the U.S. economy during the 1970s has been a matter of great concern to policymakers because of its association with inflation, unemployment, and declining real wage growth. Many possible explanations for the slowdown have been proposed, and much research has been done to determine the contribution of these factors to the slowdown. This book examines the impact of government regulation, specifically environmental and worker health and safety regulation by the Occupational Safety and Health Administration (OSHA) and the Environmental Protection Agency (EPA), on productivity growth.

Looking at data for 450 manufacturing industries between 1958 and 1980, the study finds a large, negative relationship between this regulation and productivity growth. Under certain assumptions, a large part of the decline in productivity growth during the 1970s may be attributed to such regulation. However, the study also finds some evidence that this decline could be a temporary one, representing a one-time cost of adjusting to the regulation rather than a recurring cost to society.

The major innovation of the study lies in the creation of a data set that has information on output and inputs for many industries, allowing the calculation of their productivity growth rates, along with data concerning the extent of regulation of each industry. The regulatory data are taken from surveys of the cost of compliance with regulation and from regulatory agency records of the enforcement efforts directed toward different industries. The basic result is that high levels of regulation are associated with low and falling rates of productivity growth. This result is not fundamentally changed when measures of other factors that have been suggested as causes of the productivity slowdown are added to the model.

An attempt is made to measure the benefits from regulation; this meets with very limited success due to problems with the available data. It is clearly shown that the regulatory agencies focus their efforts upon industries which are performing poorly in the areas of concern: worker safety and health, and environmental pollution. However, other results suggest that in the one area where there is a useable measure of benefits, worker safety, it is difficult to attribute significant benefits to regulation.

The book begins with several chapters presenting background information for the analysis. Chapter 2 discusses various theoretical models for productivity growth and ways to implement them. Particular attention is paid to the growth accounting model used in the later analysis, and possible problems with it are identified. Information on OSHA and EPA regulation is found in chapter 3. This information includes a brief theoretical justification for the existence of regulation in each area, a review of the legislative history of the regulation, and a discussion of the actual operating procedures and enforcement activities of the agencies. Chapter 4 integrates the material of the previous two chapters with an analysis of how the regulation can be expected to affect productivity. The chapter concludes with a discussion of models that could be used to estimate the impact of regulation on productivity.

Chapter 5 contains a review of the evidence already available on the magnitude and timing of the productivity slowdown. Previous research on the causes of the slowdown is presented, including some research on the effects of regulation. Chapter 6 sets the stage for the analysis by describing the data sources used. Possible inadequacies in the data used are mentioned, as are the ways in which these inadequacies could affect the results.

Chapter 7 presents the results of the study. A simple analysis reveals a strong negative relationship between regulation and productivity. Potential biases in this analysis are reviewed, but additional work shows that the basic result is not attributable to these biases. The addition of other factors that might explain the slowdown also does not affect the result. Further analyses are presented which do not disturb the basic result, although they do suggest that much of the impact of regulation on productivity is temporary rather than permanent. Chapter 8 considers targeting of enforcement activities towards particular industries, and offers a brief analysis of the benefits from regulation in the worker safety area. Conclusions and areas for future work are presented in chapter 9.

2

Productivity

2.1. Introduction

Before discussing the measurement of productivity growth, it would help to define exactly what is being measured. Productivity is simply the ratio of output produced to inputs used. In the simplest case there is one output and one input, both measured in constant physical units over time. If the same amount of input is used at time 1 and time 2, but twice as much output is produced at time 2 as at time 1, then the productivity level has doubled. If this change occurred in one year, the productivity growth rate would be 100 percent per year. In fact, there are usually many inputs used to produce an output, which complicates the analysis.

2.2. Productivity Models

2.2.1. A Simple Cobb-Douglas Example

First consider a simple production function, the Cobb-Douglas, and see how we can measure productivity in this context. Let output for a firm be given by inputs and productivity level as follows: $Y = ATX_1^{\alpha_1} \cdots X_n^{\alpha_n}$, where Y is the single output, X_1 to X_n are the n inputs, T is the level of productivity, and A is a constant of proportionality. If all inputs are kept fixed, Y will change only if T changes. However, we expect that input use will change as input prices change. How can we control for this in measuring productivity?

Let us assume that the firm faces competitive prices in its input markets, so that the marginal cost of each input to it can be measured by its price. Assume further that the firm faces constant returns to scale, so the α_i's sum to one. Now we can see how the firm would minimize its costs of producing a given level of output Y. It solves the following problem:

4   *Productivity*

$$\text{minimize } \sum_i p_i X_i \quad \text{subject to} \quad Y = ATX_1^{\alpha_1} \cdots X_n^{\alpha_n}, \tag{2.1}$$

or

$$\text{minimize } L = \sum_i p_i X_i + \lambda(Y - ATX_1^{\alpha_1} \cdots X_n^{\alpha_n}), \tag{2.2}$$

where p_i is the price of input X_i. This yields the following first order conditions:

$$\frac{\partial L}{\partial X_i} = p_i - \lambda (ATX_1^{\alpha_1} \cdots X_n^{\alpha_n}) \frac{\alpha_i}{X_i} = 0 \quad \text{for all i,} \tag{2.3}$$

$$\frac{\partial L}{\partial \lambda} = Y - ATX_1^{\alpha_1} \cdots X_n^{\alpha_n} = 0. \tag{2.4}$$

Combining these equations, we see $p_i X_i = \lambda \alpha_i Y$, for all i. If we denote the price of output by p_y, the zero profit constraint for a competitive firm can be written as $\sum_i p_i X_i = p_y Y$. The α_i's sum to one, assuming constant returns to scale, which yields (2.5) $\lambda = p_y$ and $\alpha_i = p_i X_i / p_y Y$. The parameters of the production function are equal to the cost shares for the inputs.

How does this help us determine productivity growth? Suppose we write the production function in logarithmic form as $y = a + t + \alpha_1 x_1 + \cdots + \alpha_n x_n$, where $y = \log Y$, $a = \log A$, $t = \log T$, and $x_i = \log X_i$. Now consider how this equation changes over time, by taking the derivative of each side with respect to time. This gives us $dy = dt + \alpha_1 dx_1 + \cdots + \alpha_n x_n$, or $\tau = dy - \sum_i \alpha_i dx_i$. The derivatives are the growth rates of output, inputs and productivity: $dy = d \log Y = dY/Y$, $dx_i = d \log X_i = dX_i/X_i$, and $\tau = d \log T = dT/T$. To calculate the growth rate of productivity, calculate the growth rate of output and subtract the growth rate of each input, weighted by its share in total cost.

The ease of the above derivation depends on the simple form of the Cobb-Douglas technology. This imposes several undesirable constraints on the firm's production function, including unitary elasticity of substitution between inputs and constant cost shares for each input. However, the same result can be accomplished within a much less restrictive framework, as we shall now see.

2.2.2. Approximations to a More General Case

Consider a production function for a firm, $Y = TF(X_1, \cdots, X_n)$, where Y, X_i and T are as before, but F is any production function which is concave and twice-differentiable. If the firm is a competitive, cost-minimizing decision maker, so that it sets the marginal cost of each input equal to the value of that input's marginal product, we get (2.6) $p_y(\partial Y/\partial X_i) = p_i$ or $\partial Y/\partial X_i = p_i/p_y$. Note that this implies $(X_i/Y)(\partial Y/\partial X_i) = p_i X_i/p_y Y$, so the cost share of each input is equal to the elasticity of output with respect to that input. Also note that (2.7) $\partial Y/\partial T = F(X_1, \cdots, X_n) = Y/T$.

If we now write a first-order approximation of the relationship between changes over time in output, inputs, and productivity, we get $dY = (\partial Y/\partial T)(dT) + (\partial Y/\partial X_1)(dX_1) + \cdots + (\partial Y/\partial X_n)(dX_n)$. Substituting equations 2.5 and 2.6 for the partial derivative terms, we get $dY = (Y/T)(dT) + (p_1/p_y)(dX_1) + \cdots + (p_n/p_y)(dX_n)$, which can be rearranged as follows:

$$\frac{dY}{Y} = \frac{dT}{T} + \frac{p_1 X_1}{p_y Y} \frac{dX_1}{X_1} + \cdots + \frac{p_n X_n}{p_y Y} \frac{dX_n}{X_n}. \tag{2.8}$$

Writing this using our earlier notation for logarithms and cost shares, (2.9) $dy = \tau + \alpha_1 dx_1 + \cdots + \alpha_n dx_n$ or

$$\tau = dy - \Sigma_i \alpha_i dx_i, \tag{2.10}$$

just as we obtained for the Cobb-Douglas. Thus the conclusion that the growth rate of productivity can be calculated knowing the cost shares of inputs and output and input growth rates is true in a more general case.

2.2.3. Second Order Approximations

Second order approximations are available, but the productivity equations become much more complicated. These approximations allow for the possibility of interactions between productivity growth and the marginal products of some inputs. This leads to the more general production function $Y = G(X_1, \ldots, X_n; T)$ which could be approximated by the translog production function

$$\ln Y = \alpha_0 + \Sigma_i \alpha_i \log X_i + \alpha_T \log T + 1/2 \Sigma_i \beta_{ii}(\log X_i)^2 + 1/2 \beta_{TT}(\log T)^2 + \Sigma_{i \neq n} \Sigma \beta_{ij}(\log X_i)(\log X_j) + \Sigma_i \beta_{iT}(\log X_i)(\log T). \tag{2.11}$$

If the various parameters of the above equation were known, and data on inputs and output were available for different years, we could calculate the level of T from the translog production function. Changes in log T over time measure the productivity growth rate. Of course, this more complex model also permits us to see what effect productivity growth has had on the marginal product of different inputs, which may be of interest in its own right.

6 *Productivity*

2.3. Measurement Techniques

2.3.1. Choice of Methods

One may measure productivity growth either by estimation or direct calculation. Section 2.2 showed that a first-order approximation of productivity growth can be achieved using data on inputs and output without estimating parameters of the production function. The second-order approximation described in the previous section does require estimation of the production function parameters. The discussion first considers how such parameters might be estimated, then turns to a discussion of growth accounting which is the principal method used here.

2.3.2. Estimation

First, let us consider how the production function parameters might be estimated. One obvious approach would be to gather data for many firms on Y and the X_i's, make some assumption about T such as a constant growth rate over time, and estimate the parameters of equation 2.11. However, this would ignore the data available on output and input prices. If we assume that the firms are cost minimizing, we can derive a demand equation for each input, based on its own price and the prices of other inputs. The parameters in these input demand equations would be related to those in the original equation, so all of the equations could be estimated as a system, imposing some constraints on the parameters across equations which would improve the efficiency of the estimation.

Another method for estimating productivity growth is to consider the firm's cost function, which is the dual of its production function. One calculates the rate of total cost diminution, rather than the rate of productivity growth, but the two rates are directly related. In the case of constant returns to scale they are equal.[1] The systems of equations used relates the cost share of each input to the price of that input and other inputs, output price, and the rate of cost diminution, which may be biased towards one or more factors. The advantage of the cost function approach over the production function approach is that the elasticities of substitution between inputs can be more easily calculated from the estimated coefficients.[2]

The translog cost function is not the only general functional form which has been proposed. Other functional forms have also been used for productivity estimation, as seen in Berndt and Khaled (1979). Some of these other production functions can test the restrictions which the translog imposes, including constant returns to scale and homotheticity.[3] It is not clear how much additional information these procedures provide, although Berndt and Khaled find that their more general function attributes a large part of output growth to increasing returns to scale. This output growth would be attributed to productivity growth if a translog functional form were used.

2.3.3. Growth Accounting

An alternative way to measure productivity is growth accounting. As its name suggests, it does not attempt to estimate the parameters of the production function. Instead, it uses the first-order approximation derived in section 2.2 to calculate productivity growth, given data on input cost shares and input and output growth rates. We cannot use equation 2.10 directly, because we observe data at discrete intervals, rather than in continuous time. The equation used to calculate productivity growth between two observations at times T and T-1 is

$$\tau_T = (\log Y_T - \log Y_{T-1}) - \sum_i 1/2\, (\alpha_{i_T} + \alpha_{i_{T-1}})(\log X_{i_T} - \log X_{i_{T-1}}). \quad (2.12)$$

Unlike the Cobb-Douglas form examined first, this permits cost shares to change over time. In fact, by using the average cost shares in each period it maintains its first-order approximation properties even if a long time period of data is being considered, during which the production function itself is gradually changing.

The major disadvantage of growth accounting is that one cannot fully test the assumptions which led to the results. When more general models are used, the estimating approach mentioned earlier can develop tests of assumptions such as constant returns to scale or homotheticity. Also, the growth accounting framework does not explicitly recognize interactions between inputs in production, so no substitution elasticities can be calculated. Finally, productivity growth is constrained to be neutral between inputs. The possibility that productivity growth will raise one input's marginal product more than another's is ruled out, and no estimates of such effects are generated.

The greatest advantage of growth accounting historically has been that it is easy (and inexpensive) to do. This was especially important before the development of standard econometric routines to do the sort of constrained estimation of simultaneous equation systems described above. The remaining advantages are related to possible problems with estimating the production or cost equations properly.

The growth accounting method allows each observation's data to affect only its own productivity value. In contrast, estimation methods whose parameters depend on all the observations allow the whole history of estimated productivity growth to be affected by each period's data. When

8 Productivity

some of the data are of poor quality (as is often the case) it may be advantageous to concentrate the effect of each data point on only that period's productivity measure.

Also, sometimes the production function must be estimated using time series data over a time period when substantial changes are occurring in the economy (as is the case here). It may be unreasonable to assume that one production function with constant coefficients fits the entire time period, as estimating procedures require. In this case, the local approximation features of the growth accounting model could provide more reasonable results.

2.4. Problems with Growth Accounting

2.4.1. Assumptions

The analysis in section 2.2 which gave us the growth accounting equation as the outcome of an optimization process made several assumptions, both stated and unstated. We now examine possible problems with the assumptions and see how these problems could affect the results.

The first assumption used (though not explicitly stated) is that all of the inputs to the production process are variable. This assumption was needed to generate the first-order conditions for the amount of each input used. If some input is not variable, or at least not sufficiently variable for the decision maker to set that input at its optimum value during each period, then the corresponding first-order condition will not hold and the model breaks down. The contribution of other inputs will be measured properly, but the calculation of productivity growth will be in error to the extent that the cost share of the fixed input does not measure the related output elasticity, and the fixed input's growth rate differs from the weighted growth rate of the other inputs.

One input which is almost certainly not fully variable is capital, about which more will be said later; but there are other inputs which may not always be used in a short-run optimal way. An example is labor, especially nonproduction workers, who are not usually dismissed during slack periods at the firm, although use of other inputs such as materials and energy is being reduced. This seems to be due to a desire by the firm to have those workers on hand when the next boom in sales begins. In this case, we would expect the input cost share to overestimate that input's contribution to output during the slack period, and the use of that input to fall by less than the use of other inputs. Consequently, measured input growth will be higher and underlying productivity growth lower than would have been calculated using the true output elasticities, rather than the cost shares.

A second implicit assumption is that the decision maker knows all the available options, which include a wide and continuous range of production possibilities. In fact, the amounts of different inputs used at an existing plant are likely to be relatively fixed, either in absolute terms or relative to the use of other inputs. The opportunity to make drastic changes in input combinations is usually available only when a new plant is built. Although there typically exists a variety of plants producing the same product with different processes, each plant is constrained in its use of inputs, based primarily on its existing capital stock.

We also made general assumptions about the context of the production decision. First, the firms are competitive, taking input prices as given and attaining zero economic profits. Second, they act to minimize the cost of producing a given output level. Third, their production functions exhibit constant returns to scale. If input markets are not competitive, input prices will not represent the marginal cost of the inputs to the firm, the first-order conditions will be more complicated, and we cannot use input cost shares to measure output elasticities. If firms are not trying to minimize cost, then all of the optimizing calculations above are irrelevant because the decision makers are not using them. If the technology exhibits increasing returns to scale the Lagrange multiplier λ in equation 2.5 will not equal p_y, and if output is growing over time some of the increase in output due to scale economies will be mistakenly attributed to productivity growth.

2.4.2. Implementation

In addition to these possible problems with growth accounting as a means of calculating productivity growth, we should also consider some problems related to implementing this method using actual data. We have assumed that each of the different inputs used in production are measured separately. In fact, we get data on inputs only for very broad classes of inputs, so that there may be substantial heterogeneity of actual inputs within each measured input class. This can cause problems when the composition of an input changes, because the input class measure used may not change while the average productivity of the items within that input class is changing (though some of this effect may be picked up in changing cost shares). We also tend to measure output by value of shipments rather than as physical output, which obscures the fact that a single firm usually produces many different outputs. The complications that multiple outputs cause for estimating productivity growth (and even defining what it means) are beyond the scope of this analysis, as are the more theoretical concerns of the existence of well-defined production functions in the case of heterogeneous inputs.[4]

Another aggregation problem faced here is the aggregation of production decisions and decision makers. The data used in this study are industry data, not firm data. Thus, each observation is not the result of optimization done by a single decision maker, but the sum of many individual firms' decisions. Depending on the form of the individual firms' production functions, their sum may not be a well-behaved production function.[5]

Despite these concerns with using aggregate industry data, there are some reasons to believe that industry production functions and productivity measures are better behaved than those for individual firms. First, there is much more scope for substitution of inputs within an industry than within a firm. Changes in the number and type of plants in an industry with many plants can permit small percentage changes in the relative uses of different inputs by the industry. Those plants using a combination of inputs that is no longer efficient given current input prices will tend to go out of business, gradually adjusting input use by the industry to current input prices. A firm with a single plant has much less flexibility regarding relative use of inputs, since its existing capital stock will constrain possible uses of other factors.

Another reason why industry productivity measures might be superior to plant or firm level measures is that individual plants and firms tend to be highly idiosyncratic. The fixed capital stock at individual plants, differing from plant to plant, makes measuring productivity differences across plants very difficult, and identifying reasons for differences in productivity growth even more difficult. When the data from many plants are added together to form industry data, such individual variation may cancel out, which could lead to better productivity statistics.[6]

Regardless of whether industry or firm productivity measures are being considered, capital is very difficult to measure properly. Physical measurements of capital (such as the number of looms in a cotton mill) are difficult to obtain and even more difficult to aggregate, so dollar value measures of capital must be used. Most measures (including those used here) value capital at its purchase price, which is deflated and then depreciated over time.[7] The capital price deflators used do not account for quality changes, only changes in the production cost of capital.[8] Therefore, adding up capital of different vintages can cause problems when quality change is occurring.[9]

The measurement of capital's cost share can also be difficult. In general there is no way to independently measure payments to capital, since they accrue to the firm itself. Rental rates for capital could provide a measure of capital's contribution to output, but these are only available for a few kinds of capital. The approach used here is to allocate to capital the entire residual profit of the firm, after the other factors have been paid. Thus, if capital is the nth of n inputs, the rest of which have identifiable cost shares α_i, capital is assigned a share of $1 - \Sigma_{i \neq n} \alpha_i$.

If some inputs to the production process are not measured at all the productivity measures will tend to be biased. This is more a question of definition than anything else. Some inputs unlikely to be measured, such as increased knowledge of production techniques or improved managerial abilities, could be called part of productivity. Some have argued that improvements in input quality should also be considered part of productivity growth. Therefore, we could (and do) define productivity as output growth unexplained by measured input growth. We should note, however, that if the growth in the contribution of these inputs to output is not reflected in the measured cost shares, it will show up in capital's share. This may overemphasize the contribution to output of an input which we have seen is likely to be poorly measured.

All of the foregoing analysis has assumed that the measured inputs are fully utilized in production. This is clearly not true all the time, given substantial cyclical fluctuations in the economy. For example, a temporary plant closing will dramatically reduce the firm's productivity measure, since no output is being produced, while the capital stock of the plant is still counted as an input even when it is not being used in production. More generally, any fixed input can be underutilized (variable inputs, by definition, will not be underutilized if the firm is cost-minimizing). This is likely to be especially important during recessions, and productivity measures do show strong cyclical fluctuations.

There are problems associated with these cyclical fluctuations in productivity. If we do not want these fluctuations to affect the rest of the analysis (in this case, the impact of regulation on productivity), we want to develop some way of measuring productivity that will not be so sensitive to these fluctuations. The most common method, which is used here, is to calculate average annual productivity growth between business cycle peaks. This minimizes the effect of cyclical fluctuations by only considering years with high utilization rates.

A second problem with these cyclical fluctuations in productivity is that they are associated with cyclical fluctuations in the residual cost share attributed to capital. By using peak-to-peak comparisons, the variation in capital's cost share is also reduced. In general, if we are looking for changes in long-run productivity growth rates and don't want the issues to be disturbed by short-term variation, we may wish to use such long-run averages rather than annual data.

2.5. Single Factor Productivity Measures

The preceding discussion has centered on what is called total factor productivity, indicating that we are interested in the contributions of all inputs (factors) to output growth. It is also possible to calculate a productivity measure for a single input, and such measures are widely used. Especially popular are measures of labor productivity, which look at output per worker (or per unit of labor input, however measured). We will now consider the

12   Productivity

relationship between single and total factor productivity and see why single factor productivity measures are so commonly used.

Single factor productivity measures look at output per unit of a single input. Let us call that input X_n, labor, and look back at the simple Cobb-Douglas model presented earlier (as before, one could use a more general model if desired). If the labor productivity level is measured as Y / X_n then labor productivity growth is given by $\tau_L = d \log(Y/X_n) = d \log Y - d \log X_n = dy - dx_n$ in our earlier notation. Since total factor productivity growth is given by $\tau = dy - \Sigma_i \alpha_i dx_i$ we get the following relationship:

$$\tau_L = dy - dx_n = dy - \alpha_n dx_n - (1-\alpha_n)dx_n \qquad (2.13)$$
$$= dy - \alpha_n dx_n - \Sigma_{i \neq n} \alpha_i dx_i + \Sigma_{i \neq n} \alpha_i dx_i - \Sigma_{i \neq n} \alpha_i dx_n$$
$$= \tau + \Sigma_{i \neq n} \alpha_i (dx_i - dx_n)$$

$$\tau_L = \tau + \Sigma_{i \neq n} \alpha_i \, d \log(X_i/X_n). \qquad (2.14)$$

The difference between labor and total factor productivity growth is the sum of the growth of each nonlabor input relative to labor, weighted by the nonlabor input's share in total cost.

Why have labor productivity growth measures been used so extensively? First, data on number of workers or worker hours is readily available in almost all cases where output data is available, and calculating output per worker is very straightforward. Second, labor is measured in physical units which have more claim to comparability over time or across firms than any other input. Finally, output per worker is relevant to issues of economic importance through its link to real wages.

The major disadvantage with labor productivity measures is the obvious one: they don't take into account changes in the relative use of other inputs. This is likely to be especially critical for a study like the present one, which focuses on differences across industries in productivity growth rates. Different industries use other inputs in very different proportions, with these proportions changing over time. Since the concern here is with unexplained changes in productivity growth, no obvious explanations for productivity growth changes should be omitted from the productivity calculation.

2.6. Conclusion

We have defined productivity growth and seen some models that could be used to calculate productivity. The growth accounting method has been chosen over the estimation method, for various reasons. Single factor productivity measures, though widely used elsewhere, will not figure prominently here. Our next chapter examines OSHA and EPA regulation, whose impact on productivity will be the focus of the empirical analysis.

3

OSHA and EPA Regulation

3.1. Introduction

This chapter describes the regulation which is considered in the empirical analysis presented later. The areas of regulation addressed are regulation of environmental pollution, through the Environmental Protection Agency (EPA) and regulation of worker health and safety, through the Occupational Safety and Health Administration (OSHA). Each area is discussed in turn, first with a theoretical analysis of the problem addressed by the regulation and then with a review of the existing regulation as it has functioned in practice.

The theoretical analysis begins by seeing what a socially optimal solution to the problem would be. Then, the reasons why competitive markets would fail to reach the optimum are examined. Possible forms of government intervention that could improve or replace the market are considered and their relative merits examined.

The practical discussion of the regulation looks briefly at the regulation as it existed before OSHA and EPA. The operations of each agency are also examined, considering both standard setting and enforcement activities. Finally, the existing regulation is considered in light of the optimum derived earlier.

The main purpose of this chapter is to reach certain conclusions about existing regulation. These conclusions are used later to develop a model for regulation's impact on productivity. First, OSHA and EPA regulation, begun in the early 1970s, represented a dramatic increase in government regulation of business activities. Second, both agencies operate by setting standards which constrain firms' productive activities. The agencies tend to change the standards over time, to base standards on technology rather than on performance, to set explicitly higher standards for new plants (for EPA), and to require extensive use of capital equipment to meet the standards. Third, it is important to consider the agencies' enforcement activities. One reason for considering enforcement is that there may not be complete, voluntary

14   OSHA and EPA Regulation

compliance with the standards. Also, enforcement resources are directed towards those firms which are likely to have higher compliance costs and poorer compliance performance.

We begin with a theoretical discussion of environmental pollution and a practical discussion of EPA regulation, then turn to worker health and safety and OSHA.

3.2. Environmental Pollution

*3.2.1. Optimal Outcome and Market Failure**

Pollution of the environment is a well-known example of an externality, a case where the private cost faced by a decision maker does not correspond to the true cost faced by society. Consider the example of a paper mill which, as part of its production process, produces thousands of gallons of waste water which it dumps into a river. Other downstream users of the river are hurt by this action, but the paper mill would not be expected to consider this when deciding how to produce paper. The problem is that there is a divergence between the private cost of pollution to the decision maker, in this case the mill whose cost of polluting is zero, and the cost of pollution to society, which includes those downstream users whose cost is positive and could be very large.[1]

Extending our attention to the entire river, there is a group of polluters who face some costs (in terms of more expensive production processes) of not polluting the water, and a group of users who get some benefits from having clean water. If we graph the marginal benefits and marginal costs of each group in terms of dollars per unit of pollution cleanup, we could get a graph like that shown in figure 3.1. Since all users are assumed to share the benefits of clean water (so that clean water is a public good), the aggregate marginal benefits curve MB is the vertical summation of the individual MB curves. Since the costs of cleanup would be borne separately by each firm, the aggregate marginal cost curve MC is the horizontal summation of the individual MC curves. The socially optimum point is indicated by the intersection of the curves. In this case, pollution should be reduced by X units, at a marginal cost (and benefit) of $Y per unit of cleanup.

How the cost of cleanup will be borne depends on whether the property rights to clean water are vested in the polluter or the downstream user. If the

---

*This section only briefly discusses the economic analysis associated with pollution. More detailed presentations are available elsewhere, including Burrows (1980).

Figure 3.1. Individual and Aggregate Benefits and Costs from Pollution Cleanup

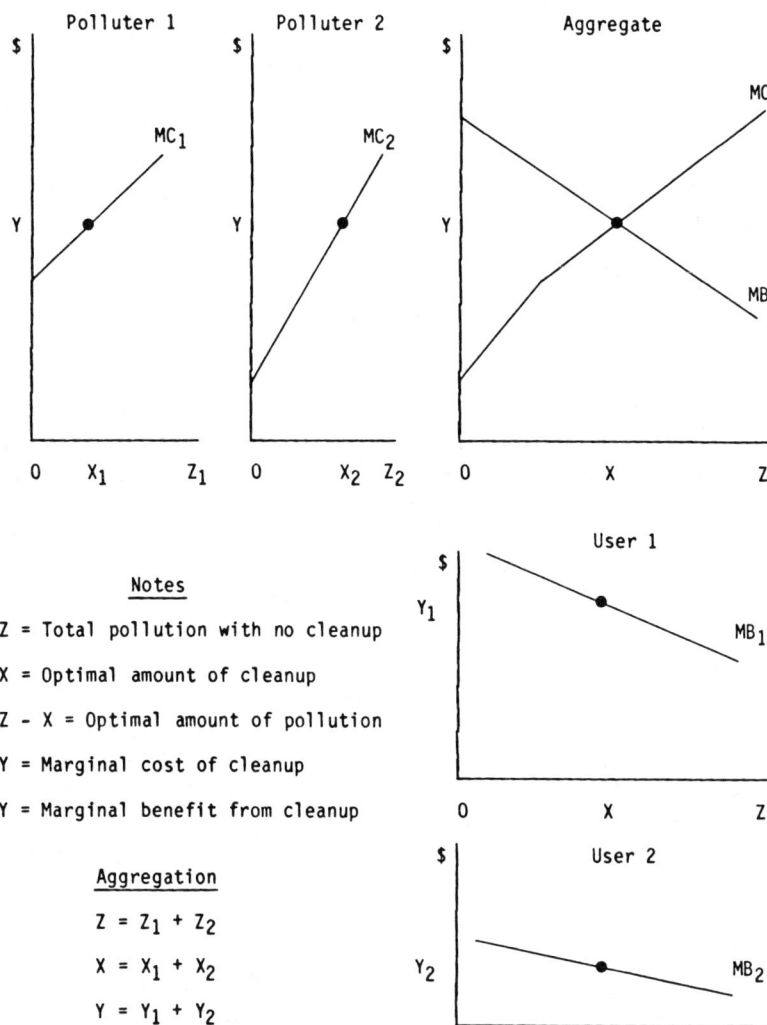

Notes

Z = Total pollution with no cleanup

X = Optimal amount of cleanup

Z - X = Optimal amount of pollution

Y = Marginal cost of cleanup

Y = Marginal benefit from cleanup

Aggregation

$Z = Z_1 + Z_2$

$X = X_1 + X_2$

$Y = Y_1 + Y_2$

users must pay the polluters for cleanup, then each user will be charged a fee based on his benefit from the cleanup. User 1 shown on the bottom of figure 3.1 will pay Y_1*X for the cleanup, while user 2 will pay Y_2*X. The polluters, shown on the left in figure 3.1, receive the same subsidy per unit of cleanup, $Y, but get different total subsidies, with firm 1 receiving $Y*$X_1$ and firm 2 receiving $Y*$X_2$.

If we reverse the property rights the same market clearing price and quantity of cleanup will be observed, but there is a change in the payments.[2] Firm 1 pays $Y*($Z_1$ - X_1) and firm 2 pays $Y*($Z_2$ - X_2), since firms must pay for the pollution that still occurs. Thus revenues collected are $Y*(Z - X). Each user would be reimbursed for the cost to him of the remaining pollution, user 1 by Y_1*(Z - X) and user 2 by Y_2*(Z - X). Whichever party is not given the property rights is worse off, and the other party is better off, with a difference of $Y*Z between the two.

One very important feature of this optimum outcome is that no two polluters are expected to clean up their emissions to an equal degree, unless their cost curves happen to cross $Y at the same X value. It is the marginal cost of cleanup, not the level of cleanup, that is equalized. Also, the marginal benefits to users will tend to differ, since they value clean water differently.

We do not in fact observe the existence of markets in clean water. A minor problem is that the property rights to clean water are not well established, so it is not clear whether users or polluters of the river should pay for the cleanup. Yet even if the property rights were unambiguously defined, few markets would arise, because of the nature of pollution's impact.

Two characteristics of pollution's impact on the users make the development of markets very unlikely here. First, large numbers of users are affected by pollution, imposing large transactions costs relative to the benefits to each user from the cleanup. These transactions costs alone are probably sufficient to prevent the market's existence. The large number of users also makes it difficult to resolve the "free rider" problem caused by the public good nature of the benefits from cleanup.[3] Second, it is usually impossible for a user to determine which polluter is responsible for a particular dose of pollution without direct monitoring of every polluter (and often difficult even with such monitoring). This individual monitoring would also be needed to ensure that any cleanup agreements are carried out. The costs of such monitoring make it highly unlikely that such a market could exist, let alone reach the optimum cleanup level, without external intervention.

3.2.2. Regulatory Solutions*

If a market is unlikely to operate to remove this externality, there would seem

---

*As was true for the previous section, this is only a brief discussion.
Again, Burrows (1980) provides more detail. Nichols (1984) examines
these different schemes in the context of regulating benzene.

to be a case for government intervention. A regulator, seeking to replace the missing market, has (at least) four concerns. First, he must figure out what the market equilibrium would have been, had a market reached the optimum, which involves determining $Y or X (or otherwise inducing the optimum cleanup). Second, he must allocate the necessary cleanup among the polluters. Third, he must ensure that the cleanup is carried out. Finally, the regulator should also consider the distributional implications of the intervention. Four regulatory schemes are presented, along with their ability to deal with these concerns.

The four potential regulatory programs are subsidy, tax, license, and standards. A pollution subsidy would pay polluters a certain amount for each unit of pollution cleaned up: a subsidy of $Y would result in the optimal total cleanup of X. A pollution tax would charge polluters a certain amount for each unit of pollution not cleaned up: again, $Y leads to the optimum. Pollution licenses would be issued to polluters, each permitting a certain amount of pollution, with licenses being tradeable among polluters: if licenses to emit only Z-X units of pollution are issued, the cleanup of X units would be accomplished and the marginal value of the licenses on the market would be $Y per unit. Pollution standards tell each polluter how much pollution is permitted: this must be set at $Z_i - X_i$, different for each polluter, in order to reach the optimum.

Before addressing the merits of the respective programs, consider the problems faced by the regulator in trying to gather information on benefits and costs of cleanup.

The first problem in gathering information is that the benefits and costs of cleanup are difficult to measure, even for the polluters and users directly involved. This is especially true for benefits, most of which are related to health problems caused by pollution. The magnitudes of benefits from cleanup are dependent on estimates of health responses to pollution levels, which can be calculated only roughly, particularly before the cleanup begins. The costs of cleanup may also be difficult to estimate in cases where significant changes to the production process are required.

An additional problem for the regulator is the asymmetry of information. Even if polluters and users understand their own costs and benefits of cleanup, the regulator may not. The participants are likely to recognize that the outcome of the regulatory process, both in terms of how much cleanup occurs and how much is paid for that cleanup, will depend on the information which they reveal to the regulator. Therefore they may have some incentive not to report the correct information, if that would lead to a preferred outcome.[4]

To implement any of the four programs, the regulator must set some parameter or parameters to induce the desired amount of cleanup. The subsidy and tax programs set a price parameter, while the licenses and standards programs set quantity parameters. Since it is unlikely that the regulator will select exactly the optimal value, given the informational problems just mentioned, it is important to know whether a price or quantity error is more troublesome. This depends on the shape of the aggregate cost and benefit curves.[5] Figure 3.2 shows two possible cases: in case (a) a small error in setting a price parameter would matter much less than a similar error in setting a quantity parameter; in case (b) the reverse is true.

An argument in favor of the quantity-based programs is that only quantity-based information is readily available to the regulator. The existing levels of pollution are relatively easy to observe, much easier than the costs of cleaning up that pollution. Since it is likely that the optimum involves cleaning up some but not all of the pollution, an upper bound is known for a quantity of cleanup parameter. No such bound is known for the price of cleanup parameter, so the regulator could set a price that was substantially above the optimal value.

Which program is best in terms of ease in setting the parameters to induce an optimum cleanup depends upon whether price or quantity parameters are easier to set optimally. This depends in turn upon the information available to the regulator, and the likely structure of the aggregate cost and benefit curves.

The second task of the regulator, allocating the cleanup across polluters, is not a problem for the first three programs. Recall that the optimum requires all polluters to have the same marginal cost of cleanup. Pollution subsidy and tax programs put a price on pollution cleanup, to which each firm will equate its marginal cost of cleanup. Pollution licenses work similarly, since the market for licenses yields the price parameter to which all firms respond. Only pollution standards require that each polluter be treated separately if the optimum is to be reached. In fact, actual pollution standards tend to be set at fixed levels across classes of polluters, regardless of differences in their marginal costs of cleanup. This leads to an inefficient allocation of cleanup across polluters and a higher cost of cleanup to society than necessary.

Pollution standards also provide less incentive for polluters to continue developing better pollution abatement techniques. Once a polluter is in compliance with the standard there is no reason for further abatement. The other three programs always provide an incentive for further cleanup through more subsidy, less tax, or revenues from the sale of licenses.

The third task of the regulator is enforcement. This requires the regulator to monitor emissions by polluters in order to detect violations, and then to punish violations. For the subsidy and tax programs, violations consist of misreporting the amount of pollution cleanup to the regulator. For the other programs, violations consist of exceeding the permitted emissions level, based

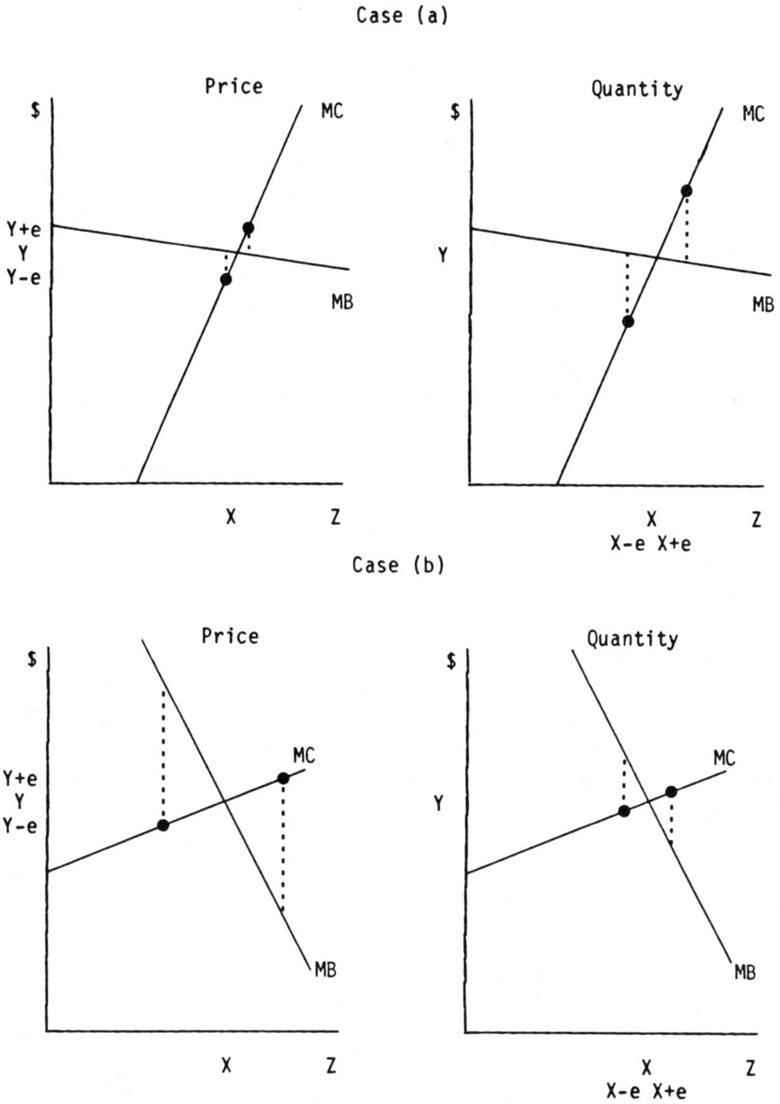

Figure 3.2. Costs of Missing the Optimum: Price vs. Quantity Parameters

either on licenses held or the applicable standards. Although the concerns are similar, the difficulty of enforcement tends to vary across programs.

The pollution cleanup subsidy has an advantage over the other programs in the area of monitoring. Polluters would be anxious to have the monitoring occur so that they could receive the subsidy payments.[6] In contrast, monitoring for the other programs offers only costs to polluters, so the polluters can be expected to resist monitoring efforts. Since monitoring will usually require some access to the polluter to place instruments on effluent pipes or smokestacks, strenuous resistance could make monitoring emissions very difficult.

At first glance it would appear that standards are the easiest to monitor, since they simply set ceilings on emission rates. The other programs require a measure of total emission, which would seem to require continuous monitoring. However, total emissions could be estimated based on intermittent samples. To the extent that occasional high emissions levels are a serious problem, continuous monitoring would be needed under any program.

All of the programs require some procedure for punishing violations, if polluters do not voluntarily comply. The principle difference among programs is that a polluter can always comply with a tax or subsidy program by correctly reporting his emissions and paying the tax. Pollution licenses can be purchased by the polluter to the extent needed to be in compliance. In contrast, pollution standards require a polluter exceeding the standard to clean up or be in violation. Thus, many more polluters might be expected to be in violation under pollution standards, which could lead to higher enforcement costs for the agency. This might be more than offset by the administrative costs of collecting taxes, paying subsidies, or keeping track of licenses. It is not clear whether any program has a clear advantage in ease of enforcement, although a subsidy should encounter less opposition from polluters.

One final concern for the choice of a regulatory program is its distributional consequences. The major difference in distributional effects of the programs comes between the subsidy and the other programs. The subsidy program imposes no costs on polluters (in fact, with a rising marginal cost of cleanup, the polluters could be better off under a subsidy than before). The standards program imposes all cleanup costs on polluters, but no additional costs. The tax program imposes a tax on polluters based on remaining emissions, in addition to cleanup costs. The license program has a net effect on polluters similar to that of standards, but individual polluters may be better or worse off than under a standards program, depending on the number of licenses they are granted. The determination of which program is best depends on the regulator's views on optimal distribution.[7]

To sum up the theoretical issues: pollution is an externality, socially inefficient because there is no market for cleanup which enables the costs of pollution felt by others to be recognized and internalized by polluters. Such a market is not likely to arise without government intervention, due to the difficulty of monitoring cleanup by individual polluters, the large numbers of beneficiaries from cleanup, and the public good nature of cleanup. Direct regulation may be less efficient than alternative programs, but the choice between price and quantity-based regulation depends on what information is available to the regulator. Finally, there are potentially large differences in distributional effects between the cleanup mechanisms, which may have a significant impact on what mechanism is chosen. We will now consider the history of pollution regulation and examine in some detail the mechanism actually chosen to clean up pollution.

3.2.3. Regulation Before and After EPA*

Before the late 1960s, most regulation of air and water pollution was done by states or municipalities. Despite a few exceptions, such as California, these regulatory programs generally did not set strict standards. They also did little enforcement of the standards, so very little pollution abatement was forced on polluters. The federal government only intervened in cases of interstate pollution, and then only by calling a conference of the affected parties, with little pressure on polluters for cleanup.

Two pieces of federal legislation in the late 1960s, the Water Quality Control Act of 1965 and the Air Quality Control Act of 1967, attempted to increase federal regulation of pollution. They were supposed to require states to develop and enforce pollution control plans. Little progress was made in developing the plans, and only for water pollution. No significant cleanup was accomplished.

The failure of existing regulation to induce appreciable cleanup of pollution led to pressures for tougher legislation. The EPA, created in 1970 to coordinate federal regulation of pollution, was required by Congress to increase greatly the federal regulation of air pollution in 1970, and water pollution in 1972. In both cases, strict timetables were set for development and implementation of standards, with the goal of reducing pollution as far as technologically feasible, without regard to cleanup costs.

The 1970 Clean Air Act Amendments changed the 1967 act in several ways, all designed to force swift action on pollution cleanup. The automobile industry was required to reduce vehicle emission levels by 90 percent within

---

*Much of section 3.2.3 and the following two sections is based on Ruff (1978).

five years. To control air pollution, the EPA was required to set primary National Ambient Air Quality Standards, based exclusively on public health considerations. Each state had to submit a State Implementation Plan (SIP) designed to meet the primary standards by 1975. The SIPs were to include land-use and transportation controls if necessary to meet the primary standards, as well as controls on industrial pollution. The SIPs were also supposed to include procedures for enforcing the regulations.

The 1972 Federal Water Pollution Control Act Amendments also removed much of the flexibility from existing legislation. The overriding goal was the complete elimination of water pollution by 1984, and (where possible) water quality sufficient for fishing and swimming by 1983. All sources were to use "best practicable control technology currently available" by 1977 and "best available technology economically achievable" by 1983. Whenever possible, effluent standards were to specify zero discharges. The EPA was to issue permits to all sources of water pollution, specifying their maximum allowed discharge rate.

Both the air and water pollution legislation set stricter standards for new sources and sources of toxic pollutants, with such sources to be regulated directly by the EPA. Both pieces of legislation also provided for enforcement of standards through court suits against polluters. The new EPA regulation was significantly tougher than the existing pollution regulation, both in standards and in enforcement.

3.2.4. *EPA: Standards*

EPA regulation has been primarily accomplished through setting emissions standards. These standards were set in a two-step procedure. First, standards for acceptable concentrations of various pollutants in the air or water were developed. There was little or no opposition to these standards since they did not themselves specify the cleanup required by any individual polluter. Opposition came later when the states or EPA had to develop a control plan to meet these standards, because these plans specified standards for emissions control by particular polluters. Although the legislation required swift adoption of the standards, adoption of the detailed implementation plans and resolution of objections to the plans took many years.

What characterizes the EPA standards? First, the standards have tended to change over time. The long delay between initial consideration of standards and final approval meant that for much of the 1970s polluters could not be certain what standards they would have to meet. Successful court challenges to standards also caused standards to change over time, often unexpectedly. The water pollution regulation had some change in standards built into it, with "best practicable" technology later giving way to "best available." Thus, there has not been a single, well-defined set of standards available for a polluter to follow.

Second, some of the standards have been written in terms of technology used, rather than setting a particular emissions level. This is most obvious in the case of water pollution where each plant is to install "best achievable" control technology. It also extends to air pollution, where 1977 legislation required that the emissions standards specify a certain percentage reduction in emissions through controls rather than just specifying a permitted emission level.

Third, both the water and air pollution standards specify that new sources of pollution must meet tougher standards than existing sources. In fact, the EPA must issue a permit before a new source of significant air pollution is allowed to start operations. Since it is usually much cheaper for a new plant to be built meeting certain standards than it is to retrofit an old plant, it could be argued that the tougher standards for new plants are designed to equalize total compliance costs between old and new plants (although it is marginal, not total compliance costs that need to be equalized for optimality). In any event, these standards do provide additional constraints on new and expanding businesses.

Finally, many of the changes in production required by the standards use substantial amounts of capital. Both air and water pollution cleanup have usually come through the installation of capital equipment at the end of the production process rather than through changes in the process itself. This may be encouraged by the EPA's willingness to view installation of the appropriate control equipment as a demonstration of compliance, regardless of whether the equipment performs as designed. The requirement that a certain fraction of air pollution emissions be controlled, mentioned above, was designed to limit use of low sulfur coal as a noncapital means of meeting emissions standards.

3.2.5. EPA: Enforcement

The enforcement process for air pollution has several stages. First, the regulator must determine whether or not a source is in compliance with the applicable standards, based on an inspection of the source by an EPA or state inspector or by certification from the source that it is in compliance (which can be checked later). If the source is in violation, the regulator (either EPA or the responsible state agency) can send a notice of violation to the polluter. If the polluter does not respond, the regulator can then send a compliance order, specifying what actions must be taken. If this is ignored also, the regulator can then sue the polluter, although limited agency legal resources and the possibility of losing the suit make this unattractive. Success occurs if the polluter agrees to a schedule for eventually achieving compliance with the standards. Of course, if this schedule is not met, the process is likely to repeat itself and another, less restrictive schedule agreed upon.[8]

The results for water pollution enforcement have been similar. A long process of negotiation leads to the issuance of a permit. Any enforcement of the permit requires court action, which the regulator tends to avoid in favor of a renegotiated permit.

Faced with large numbers of polluters, and having limited enforcement resources, both the EPA and state agencies have targeted their enforcement efforts towards those polluters which seem to pose the greatest problems. In air pollution, only those polluters emitting over 100 tons annually of a pollutant are usually considered candidates for emissions monitoring. Even among these large polluters, many are permitted to certify their compliance status by letter. This frees agency resources to concentrate enforcement on major violators of the standards. Focusing on obvious violations means that enforcement action is directed towards sources which have high costs of compliance, since sources already in compliance before the standards were issued have zero compliance costs and sources with very low compliance costs are more likely to comply voluntarily. Sources in violation, more likely to be the targets of enforcement action, also tend to have poorer emissions performance than similar sources which are in compliance. Thus the targeting of enforcement effort provides an indication of compliance cost and emissions performance.

3.2.6. EPA: Evaluation and Summary

The stated goals of EPA regulation, to clean up pollution greatly during the 1970s with little concern for the costs of that cleanup, have not been met. This has been primarily due to resistance by polluters to both standards and enforcement of the standards. If this resistance was strongest where compliance costs were highest, it may have introduced some cost sensitivity into the actual cleanup which occurred. Both the failure to achieve a drastic cleanup and the introduction of cost sensitivity may have improved the performance of the regulation, from the viewpoint of economic efficiency. Still, it is likely that efficiency could have been greater under the alternative programs (tax, subsidy, or licenses) discussed earlier.[9] Whether the benefits from the cleanup achieved were worth the costs of that cleanup, which include costs of EPA administration and polluters' resistance to the regulation as well as direct cleanup costs, remains to be seen.

The principal conclusions regarding EPA regulation are as follows. First,

EPA regulation represented a dramatic increase in government regulation of pollution. Second, the regulation is based on standards which tend to change over time, to depend on technology, to be higher for new sources, and to require substantial use of capital. Finally, considerations of enforcement effort may be important, both in inducing compliance by polluters and in providing an alternative indication of performance and compliance cost. We now turn to the regulation of worker safety and health, drawing many of the same conclusions.

3.3. Worker Safety and Health

3.3.1. Optimal Outcome: (Some) Market Success

Worker safety and health might seem on its face to be similar to environmental pollution as a public health issue.[10] There is a large population at risk, more or less well-understood hazards, and the primary "villains" are businesses: in this case for providing unsafe workplaces rather than for polluting the environment. But there is a major difference between the two. The groups involved in workplace hazards—workers and employers—are already linked through the labor market. This labor market connection could, in principle, provide the optimum level of worker health and safety protection without government intervention because it identifies the parties involved, offers a means of compensation, and has the possibility of being terminated.

The issue of identification is critical to establishing any mechanism for interaction between the affected parties. In the pollution example, an individual affected by pollution would usually find it difficult to identify the responsible polluter. In the worker-employer situation, the employer knows who would be affected by improvements in workplace safety, and the workers know who is responsible for workplace conditions. This makes it conceivable that some market-oriented solution might work. It also makes it easier for any agreement reached to be enforced, since workers might be able to observe the changes in workplace hazards directly.

The issue of providing a mechanism for compensation is also important. In the case of pollution, there would be large transactions costs associated with establishing a mechanism to link polluters and users. For worker safety and health, a mechanism already exists. Workers provide labor services to the firm and are paid a wage in return. The workers could accept lower wages to help pay for safety improvements, or they could demand a higher wage to work in an unsafe workplace. In addition, worker's compensation programs impose some costs on employers who maintain a hazardous workplace.

Finally, the possibility of termination is present in the workplace hazards case. The association between worker and employer is a voluntary one. If the worker feels that the workplace is too unsafe, he can stop working there. This may not be an attractive option in most cases, but escaping an unsafe workplace may be easier than escaping pollution.

Given the above difference between workplace hazards and environmental pollution, it is not surprising that a mechanism, compensating differentials, could evolve to induce some protection of worker health and safety without any government intervention. Figure 3.3, case (a) shows a simple model of labor supply to two jobs, alike except for work hazards. Workers prefer the less risky job (A) and are only willing to work at the more risky (B) for a higher wage. Thus the labor supply curve to job B is to the left of that of job A: if the labor demand for both jobs is the same, fewer workers will be employed at job B, and at a higher wage.[11]

If an employer could develop a technology for making job B as safe as job A (and convince workers of this), he could save $w_B - w_A$ in wages per worker. He should be willing to implement this technology if its cost is less than the savings in wages. Once equilibrium is reached in this supply of worker protection, the riskiness of jobs is optimal in the following sense. The marginal worker in a riskier job is just indifferent between his job and a safer job which carries lower pay. Mandating that a job be made safer would cost employers more in costs than employees would value the safety improvement, so it would result in reduced total social welfare.

The foregoing argument, which suggests that existing hazards are optimal and that government intervention will reduce workers' welfare, makes a number of assumptions which are to some degree false. All workers are on the margin. Only workers and firms bear the costs of work-related injuries and illnesses. All risk reducing technologies (their benefits and costs) are known. Finally, the risks associated with every job are known to all the relevant parties. Now consider to what extent these assumptions are false, and what impact this has on the analysis.

Many workers, perhaps most, are not on the margin between jobs. An upward sloping labor supply curve means that many workers on a job are willing to work at that job for lower wages than the market clearing wage. In a world where seniority governs many features of employment, including wages, fringe benefits, and promotions, most of the senior workers in a workplace could not find nearly as attractive a job elsewhere. If these inframarginal workers are more concerned about workplace hazards than the marginal workers, the compensating differential between jobs, determined by the marginal workers, will understate the benefits to workers of reducing hazards. If the employer chose to pay no compensating differential (and accept a smaller workforce as the marginal workers quit to find better jobs), some of the more senior workers might still remain, tied to the job by their accrued benefits there. This problem could be reduced if a union were present

Figure 3.3. Wage Differentials due to Job Hazards

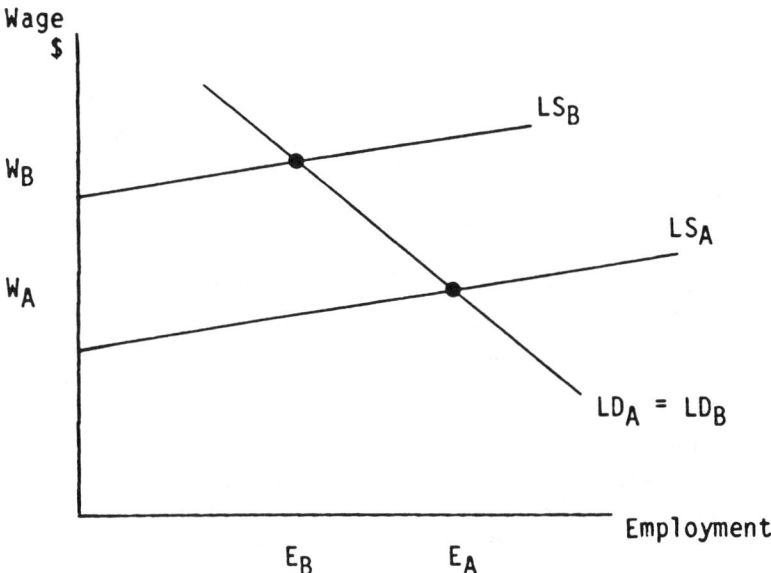

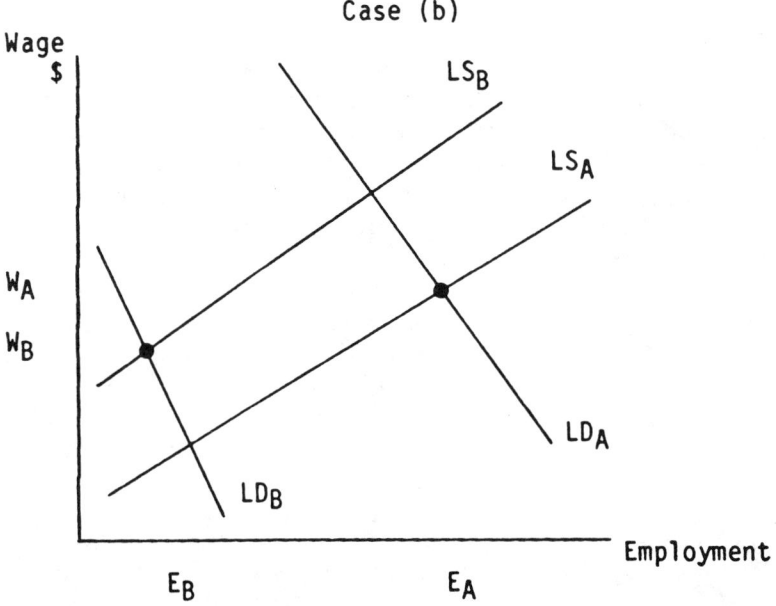

or if there were some other means for workers to induce the employer to respond to their concerns about job hazards.

Some of the cost of workers' injuries and illnesses is borne by society rather than by workers or firms. Disabling injuries or death may force the worker or his dependents to rely on welfare programs paid for by society at large. Some hospital costs may also be paid for by social insurance programs. In these cases, the complete costs due to dangerous workplaces are not taken into account by the workers and firms when the compensating differentials are established. This leads to an externality (social costs exceeding private costs), although much less than for pollution: the externality is only that fraction of costs not borne by workers and firms.

When firms have limited knowledge about what risk-reducing technologies are possible, there may be unrealized opportunities for reducing risk that would be socially optimal. The market already offers an incentive for finding ways to reduce risk, since this lowers required wages. However, additional research into ways to reduce workplace hazards could lead to improvements in social welfare.

The strongest objection to the arguments for compensating differentials is that neither workers nor firms have complete information regarding workplace hazards. The main concern here is with workers, since if they cannot assess the relative hazards of different jobs, they cannot decide what wage differentials to demand.[12] With no worker information on hazards there would be no compensating differentials, and no reason to expect an optimal level of worker protection induced by market forces.

It is not possible to establish whether wage differentials exactly correct for differences in job hazards, especially because other characteristics of jobs are difficult to measure and because different workers would value the hazards differently. There are many studies which examine wages to see whether wage differentials seem to compensate for differences in job hazards, including Viscusi (1979a) and Thaler and Rosen (1976).[13] These studies do find that in some cases people in more hazardous occupations are paid more. This indicates that compensating differentials may exist, though it does not prove that the existing differentials give optimal levels of compensation.

It is important here to distinguish between worker safety and worker health protection. The safety aspects of different jobs are much easier for workers to observe than the health aspects. This is primarily due to the long latency period for most occupational diseases. If the symptoms of a disease do not appear for twenty years, the connection between the disease and the earlier occupational exposure may not be evident. The worker will certainly not have been receiving the appropriate compensating differential for the first twenty years of work. If firms, but not workers, are aware of health hazards there is every incentive for them not to reveal those hazards to the workers.

3.3.2. Regulatory Solutions

The above discussion points out one area where government intervention is likely to be effective: the supply of information about job hazards and hazard-reducing technology to both workers and firms. Even with complete information the compensating differentials may not fully adjust for differential job hazards, for reasons given above, but at least some adjustment will occur in the labor market without requiring further government intervention.

If firms are more likely than workers to be able to identify hazards, the firm could be forced to bear the full cost of all worker injuries and illnesses. The advantage of this method is that employers would know that hazardous workplaces could lead to high costs for compensation later. Therefore firms would internalize the costs of workplace hazards and abate them if it was cheaper to do so than to bear the costs of the resulting injuries and illnesses. This would also remove any problem with externalities, such as those mentioned above. Note that if the costs borne by the firm were really complete, including payments for worker suffering and inconvenience, there would be no need for compensating differentials: workers would be indifferent between being injured and not, given the payments.

Problems with implementing such a program include the difficulty of measuring this sort of complete cost of injuries and illnesses to the workers (and their dependents). Also, it may be impossible to assign responsibility to a particular employer for an occupational disease if the victim worked for several employers over many years. This is troubling because the areas where workers are likely to have poor information on hazards relative to the employer's knowledge are precisely these health-related areas.

Additional government regulation of workplace safety hazards, beyond providing information and removing externalities, runs into problems not found for pollution regulation. There can be problems with measuring pollution, as we saw earlier. But there are far greater problems with measuring the hazardousness of workplaces, because the indexes one can measure (such as the accident rate) are the results of an underlying random process. Hazardous workplaces are more likely to have accidents, but some accidents will happen even in workplaces that are very safe, and some hazardous workplaces will go for long periods without an accident. In addition, the factors contributing to an accident often include human error, either by the injured worker himself or one of his co-workers, so it may not seem fair to charge the employer for all accidents.

Attempts to control safety hazards through standards relating only to productive equipment may be unsatisfactory because of the many factors which contribute to accidents. Not only the physical machinery involved, but also the work procedures and the care taken by fellow employees affect the safety of each worker. Individual workers with experience in a workplace will be able to make at least as effective a determination of workplace safety as a well-trained outside inspector. Written standards are likely to focus more on capital equipment than on workplace rules and can do little about carelessness of fellow employees.

Worker health offers greater possibilities for government intervention because it is possible to measure worker exposure to various substances which could lead to later health problems, and workers cannot observe these exposures themselves. The exposure levels could then be treated as pollution emissions, with direct regulation of the exposures or charges for exposures not reduced. Regulating environmental pollution is easier, however, because it tends to occur at identifiable points of a workplace such as smokestacks and sewage pipes, and is usually measured in tons of pollutants emitted. Worker exposures to hazardous substances can occur throughout the workplace, and can reach much higher individual exposure levels when only small amounts of the substance are present. This is likely to render impractical a scheme of exposure charges, since the exposures occur for different workers at different times, and really high exposures might happen infrequently. Thus, exposure standards might be the easiest form of regulation to implement.

In summary, workplace hazards need not be an externality, as compensating differentials in wages could offset the relative hazardousness of different jobs.[14] Government intervention might best be limited to providing better information on hazards to workers and firms, and correcting identifiable externalities. This is especially true for worker safety, where the wide range of factors contributing to accidents makes writing effective standards difficult and where workers are likely to recognize hazardous situations. A much better case can be made for direct regulation of worker health, where worker exposures to substances provide a more direct measure of hazards, and self-policing by workers is less effective.

3.3.3. Regulation Before and After OSHA*

As was true of pollution legislation, most regulation of worker safety and health prior to the 1970s was done by the states. Beginning with Massachusetts in 1867, individual states established agencies to deal with worker safety and passed some laws regulating particularly hazardous conditions in certain industries. These state regulations tended to be poorly enforced and excluded many workers from coverage. They also dealt only

---

*This section and the following two sections are based on Zeckhauser and Nichols (1978), with additional information from Mendeloff (1979) and Ashford (1976).

rarely with health issues. Federal regulation, with little enforcement, was limited to particular industries and government contractors.

One relatively active area for the states was worker's compensation. Although some early statutes were ruled unconstitutional, nearly all states passed some such law between 1911 and 1920. These programs compensate workers injured at work, usually paying them some fraction of their previous wages, up to a ceiling level, and permitting some reimbursement of medical expenses. Three different administrative structures are employed: state insurance funds, private insurance, and self-insurance. Contributions to either of the external insurance schemes are only partly related to the employer's accident history, except for the largest employers. End of year bonus schemes for good performance do provide incentives for reducing hazards, even for small plans. However, these incentives are only present for safety hazards. Workers suffering from health disabilities have experienced great difficulty in collecting compensation.

OSHA, located within the Department of Labor, was created by the Occupational Safety and Health Act of 1970. It was given responsibility for setting workplace health and safety standards, for conducting inspections to check for violations of the standards, and for imposing penalties for violations. These penalties could be appealed by employers or employees to an independent agency, the Occupational Safety and Health Review Commission (OSHRC). Technical information to help set standards was to be provided by the National Institute for Occupational Safety and Health (NIOSH) within the Department of Health, Education and Welfare. The federal enforcement program can be replaced by state enforcement if the state submits an enforcement plan which OSHA certifies to be "at least as effective" as federal enforcement.

Throughout the act no mention is made of costs associated with reducing workplace hazards, with standards to be set so that all workers should be fully protected from the hazards "so far as possible." Because of the emphasis on protecting workers, regardless of cost, and the provision of strong enforcement procedures including penalties levied by administrative action, OSHA represented a substantial increase in government regulation of worker health and safety.

3.3.4. OSHA: Standards

OSHA standards are set by the national office, which is permitted to use three procedures. First, standards from a large body of existing federal standards and national consensus standards could be adopted during OSHA's first two years of operation. Second, permanent standards based on research done by NIOSH can be adopted, through a formal rule-making process. Third, temporary emergency standards can be issued to cover a newly recognized hazard for six months while a permanent standard is being developed.

How has the mechanism operated since OSHA was established? The vast majority of all standards adopted were taken from existing bodies of standards. This was due primarily to the simplicity of adopting these standards, rather than developing permanent ones, and had the advantage of providing an initial set of standards for inspectors to work with. However, these standards were almost exclusively safety standards. Because most were achieved by consensus and did not have legal status before OSHA, they tended to be not very stringent, especially in health exposure levels, and included many outdated or seemingly pointless regulations that had little to do with worker protection.[15] Most of the pointless standards were weeded out eventually and were not rigorously enforced, but the remaining standards do not cover the complete range of workplace hazards.

OSHA has adopted few additional standards since the initial batch, since standards development has tended to be a slow process. Even after a long series of reviews and public comment for a proposed standard, the standard can be opposed in the courts by the affected employers. Such court reviews have often ordered reconsideration of the standard's cost and effectiveness, leading to further delays. The additional standards have shown a greater emphasis on health issues, with asbestos, vinyl chloride, and carcinogens among the substances being regulated. Temporary emergency standards have been used on some occasions, but the time required to develop a permanent standard is usually more than the six months permitted under the temporary standard.

The standards set by OSHA share many of the characteristics described earlier for the EPA standards. First, they have changed somewhat over time. This is due to both the addition of new standards and the deletion of some of the original consensus standards. The levels of some health standards have also changed over time, as new evidence of hazards to worker health has accumulated. The large number of standards imposes some additional uncertainty on employers, similar to the uncertainty due to changes in standards, since it is difficult for an employer to be aware of all applicable standards.

Second, OSHA standards, especially safety standards, are specified in terms of the control technology used rather than performance. Thus, the standard for railings might specify a certain thickness and material required, rather than how many pounds the railing should be able to support.

Finally, OSHA standards tend to favor control technologies which use capital equipment over solutions involving personal protective equipment. This is particularly notable for health standards, including noise where wearing earplugs was permitted only as a temporary solution until a quieter production process can be developed. (Recently, OSHA has reduced its reliance on capital controls to solve such health problems.) Favoring capital controls is consistent with the aim of providing the greatest possible protection, since individual protective equipment is often improperly used. However, this leads to greater use of capital and higher compliance costs than would otherwise be needed.

The only characteristic mentioned earlier for EPA standards not found here is a tendency towards higher standards for new plants. In comparison with EPA standards, OSHA standards have changed less over time, but put more emphasis on technology-based standards and capital-intensive solutions.

3.3.5. OSHA: Enforcement

The standards are enforced by inspections of workplaces, carried out by OSHA and state inspectors. Safety and health inspections are usually done by different inspectors, because the training required for the two types of inspections is different. The inspections are done without prior notice to the employer. As a result of any violations observed, the inspector can write citations, specifying the standard violated, giving a date by which the violation must be abated, and (sometimes) specifying a monetary penalty. The inspector has a great deal of discretion in awarding citations and imposing fines.

Once the citations have been issued and the inspection closed, the employer has a choice. He can accept the citations, paying the fines and abating the hazards as required. Alternatively, he can contest the citation, objecting to either the abatement date, the penalty, or both. If OSHA wants to enforce the contested citation, the citation must be sent to OSHRC, a quasi-judicial body which hears the arguments of both sides and can accept, modify, or reject the citation. The employer can further contest the citation in court by claiming errors in the standard, the citation, or the review.

With more than four million workplaces to inspect and just over 1,000 inspectors performing under 100,000 inspections per year, OSHA has always targeted its inspections towards high hazard workplaces. This targeting has changed through the 1970s. At first, most targeting was directed towards a few industries with high injury rates. Later, some industries with high health risks were added. The targeting procedures have become more refined, using yearly updates of industry hazard measures to keep targeting current, and providing lists of establishments to area offices for targeting purposes.

Employer resistance to OSHA's activities grew over the 1970s, as the benefits of resistance became better known, as OSHA concentrated on finding more serious violations which carried stiffer fines, and as the abatement of health hazards proved more expensive than the abatement of safety hazards. This resistance came at three stages of OSHA's activities. First, industry has tended to object to proposals for new standards, both during the standard-setting process and in court action opposing penalties for violating the standards. Second, a court decision in the late 1970s ruled that an employer could refuse an OSHA inspector entry to the workplace, and that the inspector then had to get a search warrant to conduct the inspection.[16] Finally, employers used the citation review procedure more frequently in the late 1970s, contesting large numbers of citations. Many of these objections are upheld, at least in part, with modifications of abatement dates or penalties. Even when the objections are rejected, substantial amounts of OSHA legal resources must be used. Further legal costs are imposed on OSHA if employers contest the penalties in court.

Just as was observed earlier for EPA, in the face of resistance by employers OSHA tends to allocate its limited enforcement resources towards workplaces where problems are likely to exist. Enforcement has been shown to be somewhat sensitive to employer resistance, but not enough to affect the positive relationship between enforcement effort, violations, and compliance costs.[17]

3.3.6. *OSHA: Evaluation and Summary*

OSHA regulation shares many characteristics with EPA regulation, and the evaluation of OSHA is similar to that presented earlier for EPA. Employer resistance to OSHA standards and enforcement precluded achievement of the original goals, which sought to reduce hazards without regard to costs, and may have induced some cost sensitivity into the hazard reductions that occurred. Both of these effects would tend to improve economic efficiency. However, the justification for regulatory intervention is less compelling for worker health and safety protection than that for pollution control, especially for regulation of worker safety where much of OSHA's resources have been concentrated. Therefore, a comparison of benefits and costs due to OSHA may be less favorable to regulation than a similar comparison based on EPA regulation.

OSHA regulation, like EPA regulation, represented a dramatic increase in government regulation of employers. The standards set by OSHA share the characteristics mentioned earlier for EPA standards, except that OSHA standards are the same for old and new plants. Enforcement effort is an important part of the regulatory process. The next chapter uses these facts about OSHA and EPA regulation to determine the likely effect of regulation on productivity.

3.4. Summary

With the founding of OSHA and EPA in the early 1970s, the federal government took on a much more active role in the regulation of business. Both agencies relied upon setting standards as their primary means of regulating. The agencies were implicitly instructed in the enabling legislation not to consider the costs of compliance with these standards. Businesses frequently objected to the compliance costs and failed to meet the standards. Each agency used a substantial fraction of its resources on enforcement in order to make more binding the constraints its standards placed upon the production decisions of businesses. The next chapter considers what effect this regulation is likely to have had on firms' production activities in general, and on productivity in particular.

4

Regulation's Impact on Productivity

4.1. Introduction

In this chapter we will examine the connection between government regulation and productivity, building on the last two chapters where we considered each topic separately. We will begin by looking at how regulation might be expected to affect firms' production activities. Then we will see how this impact would be translated into changes in productivity growth. This will first involve recognizing a possible divergence created by regulation between measured productivity growth and actual productivity growth. Later, the discussion will shift to connections between regulation and actual productivity growth. Finally, we will consider the best means of estimating the impact which regulation has had on productivity growth, both measured and actual.

4.2. Impact on Firms' Behavior

If we were to view regulation in the simple fashion presented in section 3.2.1, we would treat it as simply correcting an externality. In particular, it involves placing a negative price on an output, pollution, which is created jointly with the firm's regular output. This should lead the firm, if it was in equilibrium before, to reduce its output of the bad output per unit of the good output produced.[1] The higher the price placed on pollution, the less the firm will pollute.

The preceding view does not envision any particular problems arising for firms from regulation. It is true that their costs will rise as they are forced to pay for their pollution output. But similar cost increases could occur whenever any input's price rose. One presumes that firms would have ways to adjust to these cost increases. Why should regulation be different?

One reason is that the market price of pollution was zero before. There was no incentive for the firm to control pollution when it was developing its production processes. Therefore, the production processes may not permit reduction in pollution, or at least require major modifications to the processes to do so. In contrast, if changes in the prices of inputs were common, the firm would have had an incentive to develop flexible production processes which could adjust usage of different inputs in response to changing input prices.

In the chapter on productivity we noted that the firm's production process is not likely to be especially variable in the short run. This can make it difficult to achieve cleanup in the cheapest possible manner. If much of the existing capital stock of the firm is tied to a production technique which produces large amounts of pollution, it may be cheaper in the short run to attach a mechanism to the end of the process to clean up discharges, even if in the long run it might be cheaper to scrap the existing capital stock and install completely new, cleaner machinery.

The discussion in chapter 3 showed that regulation as embodied in OSHA and EPA tends to set standards that specify the technology to be used in cleanup. This may not produce a least-cost cleanup of pollution. More important here, it may also constrain the firm's choice of production methods by discouraging the use of production techniques that might use innovative control technologies. These constraints will tend to inhibit adjustment in the use of other factors such as labor and capital.

4.3. Impact on Productivity

4.3.1. Measured Productivity

Looking specifically at the impact of regulation on productivity, consider first the simple model which assumes that the basic production process remains unchanged. The firm is required to use some additional inputs to produce compliance with the regulation. One might model the dual output process by: $Y = TF(X_1, \cdots, X_n)$ and $C = G(R_1, \cdots, R_n)$ where C is compliance with the regulation, produced using R_i units of input i. Suppose that productivity growth is calculated for the firm without knowing how much of each input was used to produce output and how much to produce compliance. Therefore inputs and productivity are measured as $X_i' = X_i + R_i$ and $\tau' = dy - \Sigma_i \alpha_i' dx_i'$. Suppose that the fraction of each input used in compliance is given by $\delta_i = R_i / X_i'$. One can then consider what productivity growth would have been, had it been calculated using measures of "productive" inputs. Productive input growth is given by $x_i = x_i' - \delta_i$. Substituting this into the productivity growth equation: $\tau = dy - \Sigma_i \alpha_i (dx_i' - \delta_i)$.

Recognizing that the cost shares are affected little by the regulation (as long as the δ_i's are small) true productivity growth τ is related to measured productivity growth τ' approximately as follows:

Regulation's Impact on Productivity

$$\tau = \tau' + \sum_i \alpha'_i \delta_i. \tag{4.1}$$

Therefore, one would expect the ordinary productivity growth measure, which ignores the existence of compliance inputs, to understate true productivity growth by an amount equal to the sum of the cost share of each input times the fraction of that input used for compliance. To the extent that a large fraction of one input is used for compliance, that input's cost share will be overstated and the impact of its growth rate on productivity also overstated. This will not affect the productivity measurement significantly unless the productive use of that input has grown at a rate very different from the productive use of other inputs.

There is a serious practical difficulty associated with correcting productivity measures for compliance inputs. It will often be impossible to decide how to allocate inputs between the productive and compliance categories. New equipment may be both cleaner and more productive. Workers may be trained in safety procedures as part of learning how to operate machinery. Because of this, any corrections applied to productivity measures based on measured compliance costs are likely to be imperfect and could yield misleading estimates of true productivity growth.

This first impact of regulation on measured productivity focuses on measurement. The problem is not that productivity growth has changed, simply that we have overestimated the input growth rate (and hence underestimated productivity growth) by counting compliance inputs. This does not mean that compliance is costless, since the inputs used for compliance could have been used for producing other goods. However, the productivity mismeasurement does not represent an additional social cost from regulation.

4.3.2. Constraints and Adjustment Costs

One effect of regulation on firms which has already been mentioned is that regulation imposes constraints on the production processes that can be used by the firms. This could keep firms from using alternative techniques of production which are more efficient. Such losses in productivity, compared to what might have been achieved without constraints, will usually not be measurable, since one does not observe the production possibilities that have been ruled out by regulation.

If constraining the firm forces it to restructure production dramatically, we would expect to see two adverse impacts on measured productivity growth. First, when a firm changes its production process, its existing stock of inputs will not always be appropriate to the new process. If any of these inputs are fixed, the firm may be unable to stop using them, or at least be unable to stop paying for them. In the case of capital inputs, a long time may be needed before the inputs leave the firm's measured capital stock through depreciation. As long as these inputs are counted as contributing to production, input growth will be overstated and productivity growth understated. Just as with compliance inputs above, the cost of these obsolescent inputs should be included directly in the social decision of whether the regulation is socially beneficial. Measuring such "nonproductive" inputs will be even more difficult than measuring "compliance" inputs, so they are likely to be left out of any analysis of the costs of regulation.

The second impact of changing processes on productivity comes through the learning curve, a well-known phenomenon whereby the efficiency of those performing a new procedure tends to increase as they become used to the procedure. This effect may last for months or years, depending on the complexity of the procedure. When regulation requires that firms change processes, we can expect to observe a short-run fall in efficiency while workers and managers become used to the new process. The "nonproductive" input model could be extended to include knowledge of the production process as part of worker and manager labor input, and to treat this knowledge as a fixed input useful only in the old process. Either model provides a reason to expect a fall in productivity growth after the imposition of regulation, although this would be only a temporary phenomenon.

4.3.3. Uncertainty and Investment

An additional problem associated with regulation is the substantial increase in uncertainty faced by firms due to the prospect of future regulatory decisions. Part of this is because the regulator is another agent whose decisions affect the environment faced by the firm. In this respect, adding a regulatory agency is like adding another firm to the industry. The regulatory agency is fundamentally different, however, because it has different goals. Therefore a businessman will find it harder to predict the regulator's actions. Also, issues of larger policy which affect regulators tend to be political rather than economic, which may be harder to predict. For these reasons, we would expect the imposition of government regulation to increase firms' uncertainty about their future. This uncertainty will probably be greatest immediately after the regulation is enacted, before firms have any information on which to predict agency actions. The uncertainty could be kept high for years if the agency varies its rules or its enforcement in apparently unpredictable directions.

How would we expect this increase in uncertainty to affect productivity? As increasing uncertainty about the future increases the riskiness of investment in new productive equipment, such investment will require a higher rate of return to be attractive. Some investments will not be undertaken.[2] Also, firms may choose to invest in forms of production which offer more flexibility in adapting to future regulatory decisions. These flexible production processes could have lower productivity for a given input combination than other processes which specialize in that fixed input combination.

There are other reasons to expect lower productive investment after the imposition of regulation. Besides the uncertainty due to regulation, there are also delays in completing investment projects due to delays in approval of the project or issuing of licenses by the regulatory agency.[3] Firms could postpone making investment decisions until the regulator has made some ruling which affects the viability of the project. The regulations may tend to favor old plants over new, both because of explicitly higher standards for new plants and because of the technology-based standards, which may force new plants to achieve compliance by methods more appropriate to older production technologies.[4] Finally, the firm may have to do some investment for compliance purposes. If the total funds available to the firm for investment are limited by capital market imperfections, the compliance investment could "crowd out" investment in productive capital.

Why should reduction in productive investment hurt productivity growth? In principle, we measure the contribution of capital to production. Less new capital means lower input growth to offset the lower output growth. However, new capital tends to embody new developments in production technology, and the productivity of firms using new capital is almost always higher than that of firms using older capital. If no new investment is taking place, the replacement of old technology with new tends not to occur, eliminating a major source of growth in productivity.

4.3.4. Research and Development

One more area in which regulation might adversely affect productivity is through its effect on firms' research and development (R&D) activities. These activities involve searching for new products or improving the production processes for existing products. The latter, "process" R&D, is a major source of productivity growth, as it usually means producing more output with fewer inputs. "Product" R&D can influence productivity growth indirectly in the case where the product is a machine, used by other firms to produce their own products more efficiently.

Both types of R&D could be reduced by regulation. First, R&D expenditures are much like an investment by the firm in its future production, so the previous section's argument that regulation is likely to reduce productive investment would carry through. Second, the control technologies mandated by the regulations may themselves require substantial amounts of R&D before they can be implemented. If the firm faces constraints on the amount of R&D it can perform at once, some resources may be switched from productive R&D to regulation-related R&D.[5]

The presence of regulation may also reduce the productivity resulting from a given level of R&D spending, if the implementation of some of the innovations resulting from the R&D is not permitted by the regulator. This could further reduce the total contribution of R&D to productivity growth.

4.3.5. Positive Impacts

It is possible for regulation to have some positive effects on productivity. Theories of the firm that go beyond profit-maximizing behavior, such as the X-efficiency theory presented in Leibenstein (1966), suggest that firms might operate inside their production frontier when external pressures do not require profit maximization. "Regulatory shock" could act to force firms to operate more efficiently and hence raise productivity.[6] The difficulties of dealing with regulatory agencies could force firms to hire more capable managers, also raising productivity.[7] Regulation may force some marginal plants or firms to shut down, which may improve average productivity measures because the more productive firms are left behind. Finally, we should note that not all possible technologies have been used by business: a forced movement away from one method of production could lead to the discovery of more productive alternatives that were untried before.

4.4. Modeling the Impact

It is difficult to determine exactly how to model the impact of regulation on productivity, given the discussion above. Regulation may affect factor contributions to output, underlying productivity growth, and the measured amounts of factors used. We have seen that the simple approach of separating compliance inputs from productive inputs is not very satisfactory. Other influences of regulation on productivity include constraints on firm decisions, increased uncertainty, and a possible shock effect. These influences affect the use of productive inputs rather than simply requiring more compliance inputs. The measurement of compliance inputs is very difficult, which also makes the simple compliance input model less attractive.

We could view the impact of regulation on measured productivity as a two stage process. First, the measurement is affected by compliance inputs, so we should adjust input growth rates and productivity growth rates to consider only productive inputs. Then we can see whether underlying productivity has changed as a result of the regulation. Finally, we can try to determine how the use and contribution to output of different inputs changed after the imposition of regulation. This may help us understand why an observed impact of regulation on productivity took place.

A simple test for the presence of an impact of regulation on productivity beyond the measurement impact is available. Suppose that productivity growth before regulation is imposed is τ_0. Also suppose that the fraction of each input used for compliance with regulation is δ_i. If actual productivity growth remains unchanged, equation 4.1 gives the measured productivity after regulation, τ_1, as

$$\tau_1 = \tau_0 - \sum_i \alpha_i \delta_i. \qquad (4.2)$$

Recognizing that actual productivity growth is likely to change over time for various reasons, express the change in measured productivity growth as

$$d\tau = \tau_1 - \tau_0 = \sum_i \alpha_i \delta_i + u. \qquad (4.3)$$

Here u is the change in actual productivity growth, after mismeasurement due to the use of inputs for compliance is accounted for.

Now consider taking observations on compliance costs and productivity growth for many different industries, indexed by j. Restating equation 4.3, we get: $d\tau_j = \tau_{1j} - \tau_{0j} = \sum_i \alpha_{ij}\delta_{ij} + u_j$. This can be put into the framework of a linear regression model as

$$d\tau_j = \alpha_0 + \sum_i \gamma_i(\alpha_{ij}\delta_{ij}) + \epsilon_j. \qquad (4.4)$$

Here we have used $u_j = \alpha_0 + \epsilon_j$ to separate industry productivity growth into α_0, the average productivity change for all industries, and ϵ_j, an industry-specific component.

If we believe that there is no relationship between regulation, as measured by compliance costs, and actual productivity growth, we would expect the regression indicated in equation 4.4 to yield $\gamma_i = -1$ for all i. If there is some impact of regulation on actual productivity, we would expect $\gamma_i \neq -1$ and probably $\gamma_i < -1$, since most of the impacts of regulation presented in section 4.3 would reduce actual productivity.

When measures of compliance costs are not available, but other measures (say M_{ij}) of different levels of regulation applied to different industries are available (such as enforcement effort applied to an industry), we can rewrite equation 4.4 as $d\tau_j = \alpha_0 + \sum_i \gamma_i M_{ij} + \epsilon_j$. There is no longer a way to separate the impact of regulation into measurement and actual effects, but it is possible to examine the magnitude of the impact of regulation on measured productivity growth.

If we were using estimation rather than growth accounting to measure productivity, we could attempt to model directly the impact of regulation on the demands for and marginal products of different inputs, with impacts on productivity being derived as a result. As the model becomes more involved, it becomes more sensitive to possible misspecification or errors in the variables. Since compliance costs tend to be poorly measured, and are often not measured at all, this can cause problems for the more complex models. This study tends to avoid the more complicated analysis in order to get some basic results from simpler techniques.

4.5. Conclusion

Much of the existing work on the impact of government regulation on measured productivity has focused on simple measurement effects, correcting total inputs for the use of inputs in compliance activities. The preceding discussion has pointed out that there are likely to be additional effects of regulation on productivity which cannot be completely captured by measuring compliance costs, even if good compliance cost measures were available. Regulation constrains firms' activities and increases uncertainty, both of which could affect the productivity of inputs not directly used for compliance. A full model of these effects would be difficult to derive and estimate, and sensitive to errors in the compliance cost measure. Simpler models which can be estimated with available data will help us decide how important the effects of regulation on actual productivity growth are, and will provide a more complete measure of the costs of regulation. Before presenting the data and the results, we will review earlier studies of productivity growth, some of which consider the impact of regulation.

5
Productivity Slowdown: Evidence and Explanations

5.1. Introduction

Interest in productivity research has grown recently, due to the dramatic slowdown in productivity growth during the 1970s. This slowdown was more obvious because it followed a period of unusually high productivity growth during the 1960s. This chapter begins with an attempt to document the magnitude and extent of the slowdown, both for commonly used labor productivity measures and for more comprehensive total factor productivity measures. It then turns to a discussion of various explanations which have been proposed, seeing how each might have contributed to the productivity slowdown. Finally, previous studies which estimate the contributions of these factors to the slowdown are reviewed.

5.2. Evidence for Slowdown

5.2.1. Labor Productivity

The most widely observed measure of productivity is the labor productivity index produced by the Bureau of Labor Statistics (BLS). This measures productivity as the real output produced per worker-hour of all workers. It is calculated for several sectors of the economy, including the private business, nonfarm business, and manufacturing sectors.

The growth rates for this index in the private business and manufacturing sectors between 1951 and 1980 are presented in figure 5.1, and table 5.1 shows average growth rates in all three sectors for several periods. During the early postwar period, all three sectors showed impressive growth rates: between 1950 and 1969 output per worker-hour rose about 2.5 percent per year. The most rapid growth came during the long expansion of the 1960s. Some slowdown in the nonmanufacturing sector is seen by the period between 1969

Figure 5.1. Sectoral Labor Productivity, 1951–80

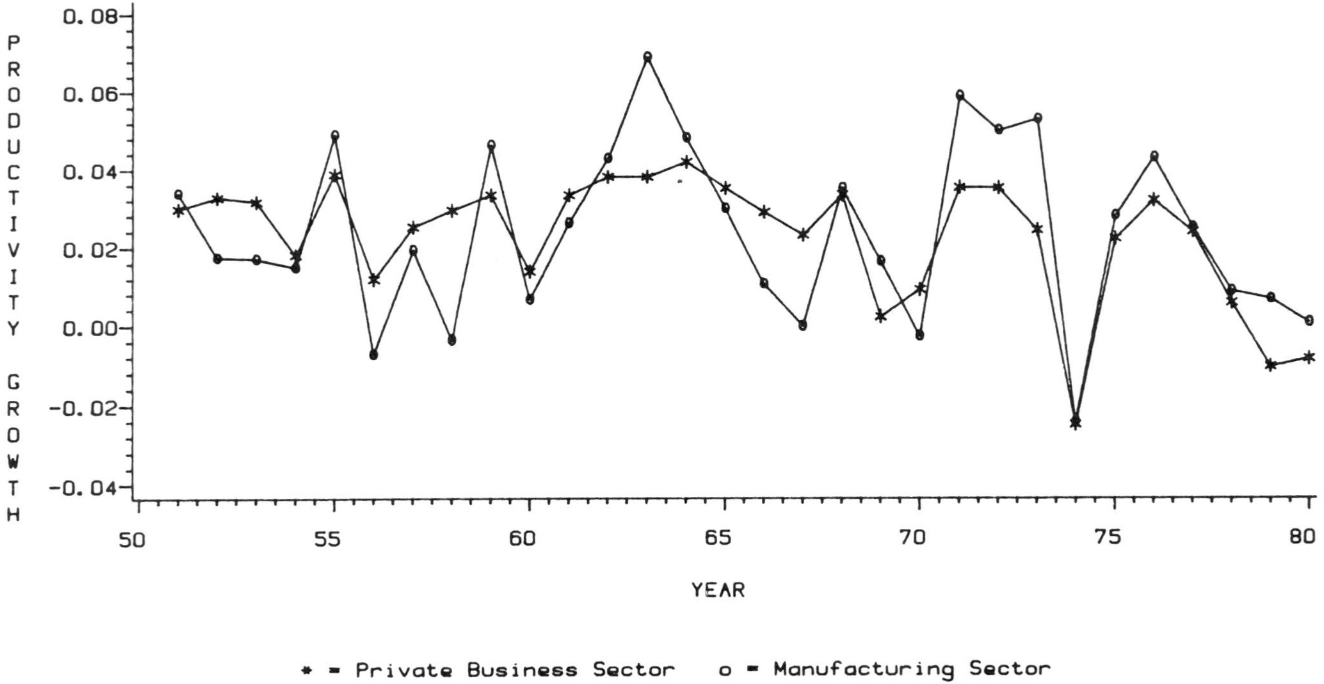

* = Private Business Sector   o = Manufacturing Sector

Table 5.1. Labor Productivity Growth Rates

(output per worker-hour)
(annual percentage growth rate)

Sector	Period: 1950-69	1958-69	1969-73	1973-80
Private Business	2.84	2.93	2.61	0.61
Nonfarm Business	2.32	2.57	2.45	0.48
Manufacturing	2.49	3.02	3.98	1.28

Source: U.S. Bureau of Labor Statistics (1983).

and 1973, and manufacturing follows suit in the 1973-80 period. During the 1970s all three sectors showed very low rates of labor productivity growth by postwar standards, dropping to less than half their 1950-69 levels.

One could argue that this apparent slowdown was illusory, caused by poor measures of output or input growth rates. Because of the simple nature of the input index used, it is unlikely to contain substantial measurement errors. Some of the apparent slowdown may be due to poor measurement of output (the construction industry is frequently cited as an example). Manufacturing, which tends to have more easily measured output than other sectors, suffered a smaller and later decline than the rest of the economy. But even manufacturing had some decline, and there seems little question that the real growth rate of output per worker-hour has fallen.

As we saw in chapter 2, labor productivity is sensitive to the use of other inputs. For example, a fall in the growth rate of capital per worker during the 1970s might account for the labor productivity slowdown. On the other hand, the labor productivity slowdown might have been caused by a real slowdown in underlying productivity growth. To see which of these explanations is correct, one needs to consider total factor productivity measures, which control for the changes in growth rates of other factors.

5.2.2. Total Factor Productivity

Unlike labor productivity measures, which use a simple and well-defined input index, total factor productivity measures vary according to which factors are included and how the different factors are aggregated to get total factor input. This leads to a much greater dispersion in estimates of productivity growth, with no single, generally accepted measure. Table 5.2 presents the results from several such studies.

These studies use the technique of growth accounting described in chapter 2, rather than using an estimated production function to calculate

Table 5.2. Multifactor Productivity Growth Rates

(annual percentage growth rates)

Author	Time Period	Total Factor Productivity	Labor Productivity
	Before Slowdown		
Griliches and Jorgenson[1]	1950-62	1.03	3.20
Kendrick[2]	1950-62	2.1	-
	1948-69	2.3	-
	1948-66	2.5	3.4
Denison[3]	1950-62	1.38	-
	1948-69	1.75	3.05
	1964-69	1.46	2.73
	After Slowdown		
Denison[4]	1969-73	1.13	2.28
	1973-76	-0.65	0.50
Fraumeni and Jorgenson[5]	1948-76	1.14	2.22
	1969-73	0.95	2.08
	1973-76	-0.70	0.31
Kendrick and Grossman[6]	1948-76	2.25	2.97
	1969-73	1.79	2.25
	1973-76	0.78	1.40
U.S. BLS[7]	1948-80	1.53	2.47
	1969-73	1.66	2.65
	1973-80	0.01	0.61

1. Source: Griliches and Jorgenson (1972).
2. Source: Kendrick (1973).
3. Source: Denison (1972 and 1974).
4. Source: Denison (1979).
5. Source: Fraumeni and Jorgenson (1981).
6. Source: Kendrick and Grossman (1980).
7. Source: U.S. Bureau of Labor Statistics (1983).

productivity growth. The output measures used are similar to those used by BLS in calculating labor productivity. The studies cover roughly the same part of the economy as the private business sector used in the BLS measures. The major difference across studies lies in how adjustments are made for the quality of inputs, especially capital.

Many of the studies were done before the decline in productivity growth occurred. For the 1950-62 period, Griliches and Jorgenson find total factor productivity growth of 1.03 percent per year, based on annual growth rates of

3.46 percent in output and 2.43 percent in input. They calculate growth in output per worker-hour as 3.20 percent per year, not far from the BLS figure of 2.84 percent per year from 1950 to 1969. The difference between labor and total factor productivity growth of 2.17 percent per year can be divided into annual growth rates of 1.72 percent in capital and 0.45 percent in labor quality. These results suggest that much, but not all, of the growth in labor productivity can be attributed to changes in labor quality and growth of other inputs. The study by Kendrick finds much higher total factor productivity growth than Griliches and Jorgenson's, primarily because Kendrick does not adjust labor and capital inputs for quality changes, preferring to ascribe this source of growth to the residual. He finds labor productivity growth rates similar to those of Griliches and Jorgenson.

Several studies of American productivity have been done by Denison. His results for years before the slowdown are similar to those of the other studies. The general conclusion to be drawn from these studies which examine data through the late 1960s is that much of labor productivity growth is explained by growth in capital per worker and increases in labor quality, but that some is due to unexplained sources, suggesting steady advances in technology.[1]

There have been some recent studies of total factor productivity growth during the 1970s, using the same techniques as the earlier studies. One by Denison extends his earlier work through 1976, showing a slight decline in both total factor productivity and labor productivity growth during the 1969-73 period, and a much greater drop for 1973-76.[2] The studies by Fraumeni and Jorgenson and Kendrick and Grossman find quite similar results.[3] The Bureau of Labor Statistics (1983) has recently begun to calculate a total factor productivity index of its own, using measures of capital and labor input. Figure 5.2 presents the behavior of this index between 1951 and 1980 for the private business and manufacturing sectors. All of these measures show that total factor productivity growth declined during the 1970s.[4]

5.3. Possible Explanations for the Slowdown

What factor or factors could have caused such a decline in productivity? As indicated earlier, this book focuses primarily on the impact of increasing government regulation on productivity—OSHA and EPA regulation. However, almost every change in the economy that coincided with this decline in productivity has been proposed as an explanatory factor.[5] Factors suggested frequently include a rise in energy prices, a long and severe recession, a decline in capital investment by business, a fall in research and development activities, and a decline in the quality of one or more inputs (especially labor).

As we saw in chapter 2, disaggregating output growth into growth in

Figure 5.2. Sectoral Multifactor Productivity, 1951–80

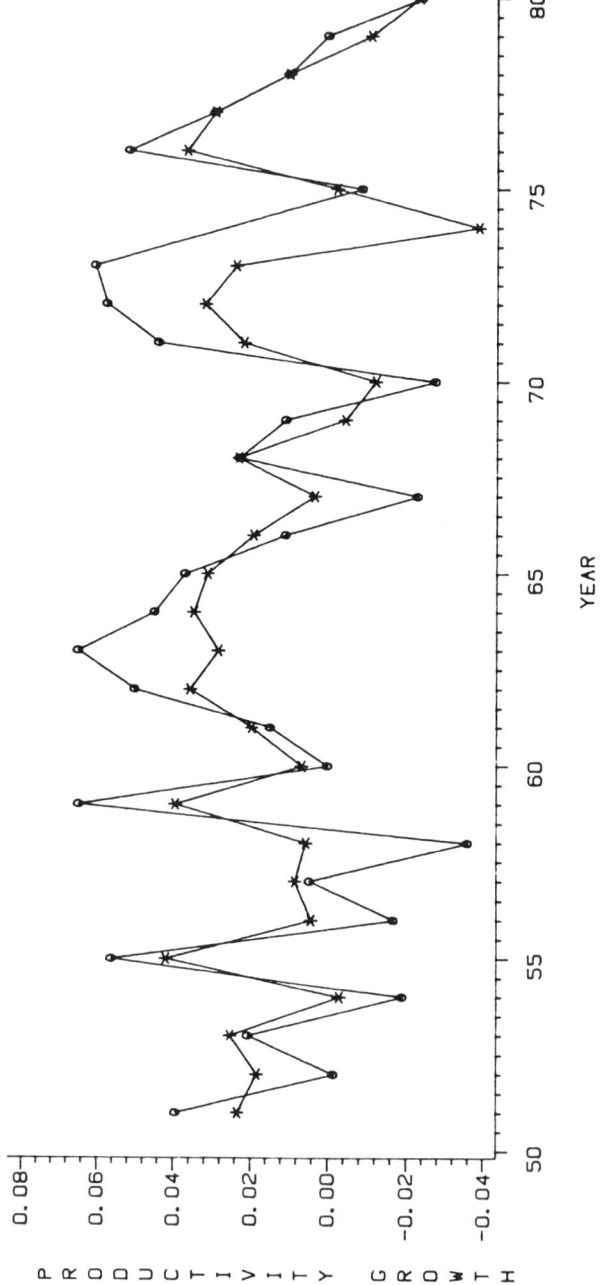

* = Private Business Sector   o = Manufacturing Sector

inputs and growth in productivity is primarily a matter of definition. Some might call a decline in worker effort per hour worked a decline in labor productivity. Others might call it a decline in real labor input and not count it as a productivity decline. Available input measures would not capture such a change in effort. If effort is part of labor input, the productivity measure is understating productivity growth by overstating labor input. Measures of effort could be used to adjust the labor input measure, reducing the estimated productivity decline. If effort is part of productivity, measures of effort would help to categorize the sources of the productivity decline. We are interested here in explaining the reasons for the decline in measured productivity: whether this is viewed as reducing the estimated decline in underlying productivity or categorizing that decline is left to the reader.

We begin the discussion of possible explanations for the slowdown with the significant increase in energy prices during the 1970s. When energy is measured as a separate input within the growth accounting model, the model does not suggest that declining use of energy due to rising energy prices would affect total factor productivity. However, the rise in energy prices forced energy-intensive industries to change their production methods drastically. This is similar to the adjustment costs imposed by regulation mentioned in section 4.3.2. Through these adjustment costs, the increase in energy prices could have helped cause the decline in measured productivity.

The poor macroeconomic performance of the economy during the 1970s might help explain the slowdown in productivity growth. We saw in figures 5.1 and 5.2 that productivity measures exhibit cyclical fluctuations, tending to increase during expansions and decline during recessions. Chapter 2 presented some reasons for this procyclical behavior, primarily the existence of fixed inputs such as capital, which are underutilized during recessions. Measures of capacity utilization tended to be low during the 1970s, confirming that some of the capital stock, although counted as part of the input index, was not contributing to output. Actual productivity growth, which considers only the amount of each input actually used in production, would have been underestimated by ordinary productivity measures.

A decline in capital investment during the 1970s has been proposed as another explanation of the slowdown. The connection between slower growth in capital and declining labor productivity growth is readily apparent. The total factor productivity measure purports to account for the contribution of capital to output, so the connection between declining investment and the total factor productivity slowdown is not as obvious. However, as discussed in chapter 4, major advances in productive technology are usually embodied in new capital. Thus, a decline in investment could be related to slower adoption of new technology and lower productivity growth. Slower replacement of the capital stock might also make it more difficult to respond to outside constraints due to regulation or energy price increases.

A decline in research and development activities would affect the discovery and spread of new technology. Such a decline could occur in response to a decline in the profitability of such activities. This might be due to a drying up of potential innovations. On the other hand, regulation could impose constraints on the use of innovations after discovery, so there might be an interaction between the effects of research and development expenditures and regulation.

Another class of explanations involves an unmeasured decline in the quality of one or more inputs. Unmeasured declines in work effort by younger workers, like unmeasured quality declines in any input, would cause measured input growth to overstate actual input growth and lead us to understate actual productivity growth. If a particular input is suspected of such a quality decline, one could examine whether industries that used that input especially heavily experienced a greater productivity slowdown than other industries.

This is by no means an exhaustive collection of all possible explanations for the productivity slowdown, but it does include the ones most frequently mentioned for which tests can be performed, given the available data. The next section reviews some previous studies which have derived estimates for the contribution of these factors to the productivity slowdown.

5.4. Previous Studies

The previous studies of factors contributing to the productivity slowdown have differed among themselves in two major respects. First, some of the studies have applied the growth accounting model directly to calculate the contribution of different factors to the slowdown. Other studies have estimated the contribution of different factors to the slowdown. Second, some of the studies have used data for individual industries or sectors, while others have used data for the entire economy. There are advantages and disadvantages to each method. Calculation rather than estimation requires less data but cannot test the assumptions used. Economy-wide data permits measurement of some factors, such as labor quality, for which no measures are available at the detailed industry level, but provides no cross-sectional variation for estimation procedures. We now review the results of these studies, saving for last those results that deal with the impact of regulation.

Denison (1979) uses economy-wide data, and uses calculations based on the growth accounting framework to measure the contribution of different factors to the slowdown. His is the most complete attempt to measure the contributions of various factors. He discusses all of them, provides estimates for some (including government regulation), and concludes that many were involved in the slowdown. He ascribes some of the slowdown in total factor productivity growth of 2.17 percent to resource allocation (.30), the legal and human environment (.30), economies of scale (.13), and other minor factors. However, he is left with an unexplained fall in residual productivity growth of 1.68 percent after accounting for those factors he could measure.

Alternative estimation techniques, without the constraints imposed by growth accounting, have found it easier to explain more of the slowdown. Weisskopf et al. (1983) find that a "social" model of aggregate productivity growth, based on work effort and pressure to innovate, explains nearly all of the slowdown. Nadiri and Schankerman (1981) manage to explain more than 100 percent of the 1973-78 slowdown in productivity growth as a scale effect, caused by the slowdown in output growth. However, an earlier slowdown (1965-73) is not explained nearly as well by the scale effect. Norsworthy, Harper, and Kunze (1979) look at labor productivity and find a similar pattern, with the earlier slowdown mostly unexplained and the latter slowdown explained largely by changes in the capital-labor ratio. Nadiri (1980) and Baily (1982) conclude that both weak demand and slowing growth of the capital-labor ratio contributed to the labor productivity growth slowdown, but also find a substantial unexplained residual. Haveman and Christainsen (1981) find a very small impact of these variables on productivity, and a large slowdown in residual productivity.

The link between energy-intensity and the productivity slowdown has also been explored. Jorgenson (1981) and Crandall (1981) find that energy-intensive industries experience greater productivity slowdowns. Bruno (1984) finds that large price increases for both oil and nonoil inputs explain much of the productivity slowdown. Berndt and Wood (1983) examine how rising energy prices might affect productivity by making much of the existing capital stock uneconomical to operate. They conclude that this mechanism, not recognized in the traditional growth accounting framework, could significantly reduce measured productivity growth.

The contribution of declining research and development (R&D) spending to the productivity slowdown is examined by Griliches (1980), who finds that R&D's contribution to productivity seemed to fall dramatically in the 1969-77 period, possibly explaining one-quarter of the slowdown. Nadiri (1980) estimated a similar contribution to the slowdown from an R&D decline. Scherer (1982) and Griliches and Lichtenberg (1984) do not find evidence for the disappearance of R&D's contribution to productivity growth, although declining R&D could still contribute to the productivity slowdown.

The principal explanation for the productivity slowdown considered here is government regulation, done by OSHA and EPA. Studies which calculate the contribution of regulation to the slowdown based on compliance cost estimates tend to produce small estimates. Denison (1979) estimates that such regulation contributed .35 percent to the productivity slowdown in the

1972-75 period, and in a later study (1983) concludes that the contribution fell to .15 percent in the 1973-81 period. Portney (1981) notes that little of Gross National Product (GNP) is spent on pollution control (under 2 percent).

Estimates, using cross-industry or time-series data, have generally given slightly larger, but similar results. Norsworthy, Harper, and Kunze (1979) find that pollution abatement capital had a limited effect on labor productivity. Scherer (1982) finds that pollution and health and safety investment reduced productivity growth by .19 to .27 percent, but this effect is not significant. Kendrick (1983) finds that measures of regulation were not significantly related to variation in total factor productivity growth across 20 manufacturing sectors. Using time-series data and measures of total federal regulation, Christainsen and Haveman (1981) find regulation responsible for about 20 percent of the slowdown. Crandall (1981) finds a strong relationship between pollution abatement capital and productivity, but this relationship disappears when a measure of energy intensity is included. Using time-series data, Siegel (1979) observes a significant contribution (.5 percent) from pollution control expenditures to the productivity slowdown for 1965-73, but not for later years. Pashigian (1984) compares industries that differ on pollution abatement costs, finding falling numbers of plants and labor's share in total cost, but rising value-added for high abatement cost industries. Finally, Gollop and Roberts (1983) examine data for a set of electric utilities and find that regulation of emissions had a large impact on total factor productivity, lowering it for regulated firms by .59 percent. The conclusion of these studies (except perhaps for Gollop and Roberts) is that pollution abatement costs in particular, and regulation in general, explain about 10 percent of the productivity slowdown.

5.5. Summary

There are four general conclusions to be reached from the previous work presented here. First, there was a productivity slowdown during the 1970s, at least in measured productivity. Second, many different factors seem to have contributed to it, to different degrees. Third, government regulation contributed a small but potentially significant amount to the slowdown. Fourth, a sizeable fraction of the slowdown remains unexplained by the estimated contributions of all the factors considered. We now proceed to the empirical analysis in chapter 7, after discussing the data sources used.

6
Data Description

6.1. Introduction

The data set used in this analysis consists of data for 450 manufacturing industries at the 4-digit level, based on the 1972 Standard Industrial Classification (SIC).[1] Annual data from 1958 to 1980 on real and nominal output and inputs are used in the calculation of industry productivity growth. Data are also available on the extent of government regulation of these industries for the more recent years of the period (as we saw in chapter 3, there was relatively little regulation before the early 1970s). Additional data include information on research and development spending and measures of industry performance on pollution abatement and protection of worker safety and health. The major data sources are listed in table 6.1. We now turn to a detailed description of each type of data and the way in which they are combined.

6.2. Productivity Data

The principal source of the data needed to calculate productivity growth was a joint project by the University of Pennsylvania, the Bureau of the Census, and SRI, Inc. This project assembled basic input and output data from 1958 to 1976 on all 450 industries. It is referred to here as the PCS data set.[2] Much of this data, including inputs, outputs, and factor shares, was taken from the Annual Surveys of Manufactures and Censuses of Manufactures. The major contribution of the project was the development of measures of the real capital stock of each industry, using data on the composition of investment goods purchased by each industry. Price deflators for shipments, materials, energy, and investment were also developed. We will consider the derivation of the data, problems with it, and the methods used to revise and update the PCS data to put it in final form for this study.

The Annual Survey of Manufactures (ASM) collects data from about 120,000 manufacturing establishments, chosen in a stratified random sample

56 Data Description

Table 6.1. Major Data Sources

Source	Period	Data
Productivity Sources		
U Penn - Census - SRI	1958-1976	Output, inputs, prices
Census of Manufactures	1977	Output, inputs
Annual Survey of Manufactures	1978-1980	Output, inputs
Regulation Sources		
McGraw-Hill Safety Investment Survey	1973-1980	Investment in worker health and safety
Census - Pollution Abatement Costs Survey	1973-1980	Pollution control capital and operating costs
OSHA Management Information System	1972-1980	OSHA inspections, citations
EPA Compliance Data System	1970-1980	EPA enforcement actions
Other Data Sources		
Scherer - R+D cross-sectional data	1977	R+D expenditures
NIOSH Injury Survey	1958-1970	Injury rates
BLS Occupational Injuries and Illness Survey	1972-1979	Injury rates
OSHA Industry Priority Report	1981	Health hazard rankings
EPA National Emissions Data System	1970-1980	Emission levels, control equipment efficiencies

based on employment size, with establishments employing 500 or more workers certain to be sampled. Every five years a Census of Manufactures (COM) collects data from all manufacturing establishments with more than 10 employees which is used to help revise the ASM sample and its weighting procedure. The data collected include number of employees, number of and hours worked by production employees, and dollar values for total shipments, value added, total payroll, production worker wages, end-of-year inventories, materials used, energy used (available since 1972), and investment spending on new plant and equipment.

Each establishment is classified into a 4-digit industry based on its primary product. For many establishments this can cause problems, especially in manufacturing where a large establishment frequently produces dozens of products. Although the products are usually similar, it is not unusual to see several 4-digit product classes present. If so, the establishment is assigned to the 4-digit industry whose product class represents the largest share of the establishment's total output by value. In order to avoid having establishments change industry in every census year due to minor changes in product mix, large changes in product mix are required to change the industry classification of an existing establishment. The fraction of each 4-digit product's total output accounted for by that 4-digit industry is the coverage ratio, which averages 87 percent and is as low as 25 percent.[3] The specialization ratio measures the share of the 4-digit industry's output accounted for by that 4-digit product, averages 90 percent, and is as low as 61 percent.[4] This or any establishment-based classification will be imperfect, but better than a firm-based data set where many different establishments from the same firm would have to be classified into the same industry.

Industry totals are reported for each variable at the 4-digit level. The Census Bureau will not publish data for industries where very few establishments exist (to avoid disclosing data for a particular establishment), or where the data are believed to be of especially poor quality. This occurred frequently in the earlier years of the data, but is not a problem for data after 1972. Virtually all of the data is available in census years (1958, 1963, 1967, 1972, and 1977) because of the complete sample taken in those years.

One problem faced in dealing with the data is how to fill in these missing values when they occur. The method used in the PCS project is not obvious from the data set, and occasionally it seemed to produce large yearly fluctuations in some variables but not in other, closely related, variables. Alternative estimates for missing values were produced from the original ASM data by the following procedure. First, values for all variables were obtained at the 2-digit industry level. This required imputing very few values, which was done based on values of that variable for surrounding years and for related variables in that year. Then, all variables were obtained at the 3-digit industry level. Missing values of a variable for a 3-digit industry were imputed by calculating the sum of that variable (if present) for the other 3-digit industries within the same 2-digit industry. This sum was subtracted from the 2-digit value. The remainder was allocated among those 3-digit industries with missing values, based on the relative sizes of those industries' values in surrounding years. The procedure was repeated to fill in missing 4-digit industry data, based on the 3-digit data.

To check the imputation results for reasonableness, as well as to look for anomalous values in the original ASM and COM data, a series of tests was run on the data set. First, those cases where one variable should always be greater than another (such as total employees and production workers or value of shipments and value added) were checked. Then ratios of variables (such as production workers to total employees) that should stay roughly constant over time were checked for wild fluctuations in values. The values of the variables themselves were also checked for fluctuations, although for some variables such as inventories these fluctuations are not unusual. A few problem cases were found in the ASM data. These were checked against the original, published ASM data. A few values that seemed completely aberrant were changed directly, based on values for that variable in surrounding years.[5] The results from this procedure were used in cases where the PCS data seemed to have difficulties with imputation.

Another problem which has to be dealt with is the redefinition of the SIC codes, which occurs to a greater or lesser degree in each census year. By far the largest redefinition occurred in 1972. Many industries were not changed at all, and many more industries had their SIC codes changed but retained their identity. However, a large number of 4-digit industry definitions were fundamentally changed, with some 1967 industries being split among 2 or more 1972 industries and some 1972 industries made up of pieces from several 1967 industries.

Fortunately, the Census Bureau does provide measures of how much of each 1967 industry went into each 1972 industry. These data are obtained by looking at those establishments whose industry was changed by the SIC code revisions (based on the primary product of the establishment). The figures are given in terms of both total employees in the establishments which changed industry and value added in those establishments. The earlier data from 1958 to 1971 was reapportioned, based on the value added measure. That is, if a 1967 SIC industry was split into two 1972 SIC industries, with one piece accounting for 60 percent of the value added and the other for 40 percent, all of that industry's variables for all of the years before 1972 would be split into two pieces, with 60 percent allocated to one 1972 SIC and 40 percent to the other.

This scheme is easy to implement, and can be applied to other data sets. An alternative scheme, getting the allocation fractions separately for each variable, would have avoided the assumption implicit here that each piece of the 1967 SIC industry contains the same fraction of all the variables. However, this would have required getting additional data from the Census Bureau, would not have been applicable to other data sets, and would still have required the assumption that the relative sizes of the 1967 SIC industry pieces did not change during the period between 1958 and 1971. Besides, changes to the PCS data were generally avoided unless they were clear improvements.

Calculating real capital stock for each industry was the focus of the PCS project. First, the ASM investment data were disaggregated into several investment categories. For each category, depreciation rates and price deflators were obtained. This enabled the calculation of real investment and depreciation, given nominal investment and real capital stock in each category. Old real capital stock plus new real investment minus depreciation of old capital yielded new real capital stock. This was done from year to year through the period. Because of the intricate nature of these calculations and the large number of outside data sources used, no attempt was made here to check or correct the PCS capital stock data.

Price deflators were needed for the variables measured only in dollar terms on the ASM. These deflators were taken from more recent sources than those used in the PCS data. Deflators for the value of shipments were obtained for each industry from the Bureau of Industrial Economics in the Commerce Department. Energy price deflators were calculated for each industry, based on Bureau of Labor Statistics price indexes for six types of energy, weighted by the industry's relative use of each type. Materials deflators were also constructed for each industry. The 1972 Input-Output Tables provided a detailed breakdown of an industry's purchases from each of the other 449 4-digit manufacturing industries and 135 nonmanufacturing industries. Output price indexes from BLS for other manufacturing and nonmanufacturing industries were aggregated for each of the 450 industries, using weights based on that industry's purchases from the other industries, to yield a price deflator for the cost of materials.

The PCS data was then updated through 1980. Data from the 1977 COM and 1978 through 1980 ASMs provided the basic production information. The real capital stock data was extended for four years, using investment data from the ASM and capital stock and investment deflator data from the Bureau of Industrial Economics in the Commerce Department. The various price deflators created for this study were available through 1980. The capital stock measure is the only one which is constructed differently before and after 1976, but since an industry's capital stock changes fairly slowly over time this shouldn't affect the results found later.

In summary, there are some problems with this data. The usual problems of misunderstood questions, data entry errors, and nonrepresentative samples are reduced here by the large sample size and the Census Bureau's error-checking procedures. The major difficulty with comparability over time comes from SIC industry definition changes, most obviously in 1972. The capital stock data may suffer from problems with deflators and depreciation rates for investment categories, as well as the usual problems encountered whenever one tries to measure capital. The price deflator data have some difficulty coping with rapid changes in product quality over time. Despite all

60   Data Description

of these problems, this represents the best data available on such a level of industry detail and should yield productivity measures which are of reasonable quality.

6.3. Regulation Measures: Compliance Costs

6.3.1. OSHA

There is very limited data on costs to firms of complying with OSHA regulation. Some compliance cost estimates are generated whenever OSHA proposes a new standard, since the standards review process includes some cost considerations. These estimates sometimes disaggregate compliance costs by industry, although this is not done on a consistent basis across standards. More importantly, such estimates are not made for old standards and there is no source that collects all such cost estimates in a form useable for cross-industry comparisons.

The data we do consider are taken from an annual McGraw-Hill survey on capital spending for the 1973 to 1980 period. Each year McGraw-Hill collects information from a few hundred large firms on current-year capital expenditures and projected expenditures for the next year and for two years later. These data include questions on both the amount and the composition of capital spending.

One question asks what fraction of total capital spending is allocated to worker safety and health. Problems with this data include the nonrepresentative nature of the firms sampled, the low response rate (especially on the safety and health question), and the small size of the total sample. The small sample forces the data to be presented in an very aggregate form, with only 16 industry sectors identified in manufacturing. All 4-digit SIC industries within each sector had to be assigned the same value. These data are examined briefly in chapter 7, but they prove unsatisfactory due to the problems mentioned here.

6.3.2. EPA

The data for pollution abatement costs were also taken from a survey, but this survey was superior to that used for OSHA-related costs. These data are from the Pollution Abatement Costs and Expenditures Survey, taken annually by the Bureau of the Census since 1973. The survey is sent to about 20,000 establishments, a subsample of those in the Annual Survey of Manufactures excluding establishments in major group 23.[6]

The survey asks respondents to report capital expenditures and operating costs for pollution abatement, disaggregated by type of pollutant abated and type of cost. For example, operating costs are divided into depreciation, labor, equipment leasing, and other costs. There is some question about whether the respondents have enough information to distinguish between the types of costs, and the few attempts made to utilize these distinctions in the analysis were not successful. In addition, there was apparently a major problem with respondents not understanding the questionnaire at all during the 1973 survey, so the 1973 data are not used often in the analysis.

The data are reported for 2-, 3-, and 4-digit SIC industries. These values are not presented by the Census Bureau for every 4-digit industry in a given year, either for reasons of data quality or to avoid disclosing data from individual establishments. Most of the pollution abatement costs are concentrated in a few industries, and these data are usually present in each year. In order to fill in the missing values a process similar to that described earlier for the ASM data was used. After getting values for all 2-digit SIC industries, missing 3-digit values were filled in based on their relative sizes in nearby years. The process was repeated to generate complete 4-digit data. Because most of the missing industries spent little for pollution abatement, a fairly small amount of the total costs were allocated, but many industries had missing values filled in by this procedure.[7]

The data was then checked for unusual fluctuations. Many fluctuations might have been caused by the process used to allocate missing variables. However, even when data was present for an industry over several years, there were still large fluctuations, especially when one considered percentage changes. This could cause some problems for any yearly change analysis, providing a reason to use average pollution abatement expenditures over several years to compare industries, rather than using annual data. Since most of the missing values are for industries with small values for pollution abatement spending, one approach used in chapter 7 is to drop all industries with average pollution abatement operating cost under $1.0 million.

6.3.3. Common Concerns

One problem for both the EPA and the OSHA compliance cost measures is that they don't measure the incremental cost of complying with the new regulations. If firms, for some reason, had been spending money to clean up pollution before EPA existed, this survey of total pollution abatement costs will overstate the additional burden imposed by EPA. A more general problem with both surveys is that it is very difficult to measure compliance costs, especially when considering costs of new production processes or equipment that is both cleaner, safer, and more productive.

As we saw in chapter 4, we should express inputs used for compliance as a fraction of the total use of that input. Capital expenditures for compliance are deflated by the new investment price deflator and then divided by real capital stock to express them as a share of real capital input. Operating costs are more difficult to allocate to a particular input, but most of the operating costs would count as materials cost on the ASM data, so operating costs for compliance are expressed as a fraction of total materials cost. Now we consider another way of measuring regulatory impact: the enforcement activities of the agencies.

6.4. Regulation Measures: Enforcement

6.4.1. OSHA

To measure OSHA enforcement efforts we have a copy of OSHA's Management Information System (MIS) database, which contains a record of all OSHA inspections carried out from late 1972 to 1980. There are 538,796 inspections recorded on the data set, of which 256,905 are inspections of manufacturing establishments. Because this database is used by OSHA to track its enforcement effort, the inspectors are required to enter all inspections into the MIS system. Each inspection record includes date, 4-digit SIC code, number of employees, and information on citations and penalties.

Any enforcement measure which we generate from this data must be an industry- and nation-wide one to permit its use with the industry-and nation-wide data on productivity. This aggregation is possible because the SIC industry code on the MIS data is given at a 4-digit level. Assigning an establishment to a particular industry may be difficult for multiproduct establishments, as was mentioned above in connection with the ASM data. In the case of the MIS, the industry assignments are done by trained inspectors, so they should be no less accurate than the ASM industry assignments.

The only major problem with using the data was created when the MIS changed from the 1967 SIC codes to the 1972 SIC codes. This change occurred in 1975. All previous inspections were allocated to the appropriate new code, except when one 1967 SIC code split into two or more 1972 SIC codes. In that case the inspection was assigned the 3-digit SIC code from which the multiple 1972 SIC 4-digit codes came. These inspections are allocated among the appropriate 1972 SIC 4-digit codes, based on relative numbers of inspections in the industries after 1976. In a few cases 3- or 2-digit codes were used after 1975 rather than the 4-digit codes which were supposed to be used. The 3-digit inspections are allocated among the valid 4-digit industries, based on the number of inspections recorded in those industries, and the 2-digit inspections are ignored. Out of over 250,000 manufacturing inspections, only 7,106 needed to be allocated and only 92 could not be allocated to a valid 4-digit industry.

As was noted in chapter 3, there are "state plan" states that use their own enforcement programs rather than OSHA's. In some cases this data is entered on the MIS, and OSHA does do some inspections in all states. However, to the extent that different industries are located more or less in states which do not enter their data on the MIS, the MIS-based enforcement measures may over- or understate the relative enforcement effort directed at different industries. No attempt to correct for this is made because the productivity data could only be calculated on a nationwide basis.

The two enforcement measures used in this analysis are annual inspection rates for each industry. The simpler measure takes the number of inspections in an industry and divides that by the number of establishments in the industry. Because the size of plant inspected (number of employees) is also available, an alternative measure can be constructed. This weights each inspection by the number of employees in the establishment and divides the total by the number of employees in the industry. An inspection of a larger plant generally takes more inspector time, has more citations, and affects a larger fraction of total industry output than an inspection of a smaller plant. Any tendency to inspect larger plants in one industry than another would be captured by this employee inspection rate but not by the establishment inspection rate, although in practice the two measures are closely correlated.

6.4.2. EPA

The enforcement data available for EPA from the Compliance Data System (CDS) is not as comprehensive as the OSHA MIS data. It is also less critical for the research, since the EPA compliance cost data is much better than that for OSHA. The major problem is that the CDS contains only air pollution enforcement data. There is no comparable enforcement data available for water pollution. Also, the bulk of the air pollution regulations are contained in the SIPs prepared by each state, with both standards and enforcement varying across states. Not all states participate fully in the CDS data maintenance. The EPA records its own enforcement of national standards such as NSPS and NESHAPS on the CDS.

The unit of observation for the CDS data is the establishment, rather than the inspection. There are 29,216 manufacturing establishment records on the CDS (out of 49,087 total), of which most are large plants subject to SIP regulations and the rest are subject to regulation by EPA directly, through NSPS or NESHAPS. The SIC code of the establishment is identified. Its current compliance status with respect to major pollutants is indicated. All enforcement actions directed at that establishment are found on the record, with information on the type of action and the effective date. Not all actions are inspections, with letters, hearings, and other noninspection events accounting for the majority of actions.

The 1972 change in SIC codes must have forced the reassignment of some nents, but the procedure used is not as clear as that used in the IIS data. There are also some invalid SIC codes present, and more use of 2- and 3-digit codes than found on the MIS. Establishments were allocated among closely related valid 4-digit codes when this was possible. Most establishments did not require allocation, but the allocation procedure had a higher error rate than that for the MIS.[8]

Since enforcement actions come in many different types, it is possible to get many different measures of enforcement rates, although the measures tend to be highly correlated across industries. The annual inspection rate was calculated as the number of federal and state inspections of an industry divided by the number of establishments in that industry. An enforcement action rate, which counted the total number of actions rather than inspections only, was also calculated. Its major problem is that it treats all actions alike, ranging from "letter sent" to "federal inspection." The action rate was tested briefly, but the analysis presented later uses only the inspection rate measure.

6.4.3. General Usefulness

Why use enforcement measures? In chapter 3 we saw the importance of enforcement in any analysis of regulation. Without any enforcement of regulation, it is not generally in the interest of firms to comply with the regulation. Neither EPA nor OSHA regulation has been uniformly obeyed by firms. Some of this may be due to firms misunderstanding the rules, but there are many cases where firms deliberately violate the rules, either because that is cheaper than complying with the rules or to convince the regulatory agency to change the rules.

We expect the enforcement effort from each agency for an industry to be positively correlated with the compliance cost imposed by the regulation on that industry. Each agency engages in some targeting of inspections and other compliance activities towards those industries which are performing poorly, with high accident rates or pollution emissions. These industries are those which face the highest compliance costs. There may be some tendency for the agencies to avoid enforcement in high compliance cost industries because those industries are more likely to resist the regulations. However, the data show a tendency for high enforcement industries to have high compliance costs and to perform poorly on measures of compliance with regulation.

If we had exact and complete measures of compliance costs imposed by regulation, enforcement measures might not be necessary to measure the impact of regulation on productivity. However, we have seen that perfect measures of compliance costs are difficult or impossible to obtain, due to problems with separating the use of inputs in production from compliance usage. The measure we do have of the costs of complying with worker health and safety regulation is inadequate, and the measure of pollution abatement costs may have some problems. We have enforcement data for both OSHA and EPA regulation, and this data can be used to supplement or replace the compliance cost data.

6.5. Other Data Sets

Besides the major data sets on productivity and regulation described above, several other data sets also listed in table 6.1 are used in the analysis. Data on research and development (R&D) spending by industry provide possible controls for the rate of technological change in an industry. Measures of hazards faced by workers, both safety and health related, are needed to check for targeting of OSHA inspections towards hazardous industries. Data on pollution emissions and control technology permit testing for targeting of EPA enforcement actions. These data sets are described briefly below.

Data on R&D expenditures for 193 manufacturing industry aggregates are taken from Scherer (1981). These data include measures of R&D spending by industry, the percentage of all industry patents that relate to the production process (rather than to new products), and measures of R&D used by industry, including R&D done by other industries.[9] R&D spending by the industry and total R&D used by the industry are the measures examined in the analysis. Each is divided by the total industry capital stock to adjust for differences in industry size. Because these data are in cross-section form and not time-series, we cannot use changes in R&D spending to explain changes in productivity growth, but we can examine whether differences in R&D spending across industries seem to be associated with different rates of productivity growth.

The industry accident rate data is taken from two data sets, a NIOSH survey between 1958 and 1970 and a BLS survey between 1972 and 1979. Although both surveys are similar, the accident measures differ slightly (the BLS only counts accidents which resulted in lost workdays). Also, the NIOSH record keeping procedure was voluntary, while all firms are now required to maintain records in the BLS-specified format. The lack of overlap between the NIOSH and BLS data makes it difficult to adjust the two series to make them comparable. The BLS values are roughly three times as large as the NIOSH values, so the NIOSH values were inflated by a factor of three when direct comparison was needed. Comparability also suffers from the major revision of SIC codes in 1972. The NIOSH data for 1967 SIC industries are allocated among 1972 SIC industries, based on industry value-added, assuming that all parts of a given 1967 SIC industry had the same accident rate. Despite comparability problems over time, this data does let us look at changes in industry accident rates over time, as well as the relative hazards to workers in different industries.

The OSHA Industry Priority Report ranks 309 4-digit industries, based on worker exposure to health hazards and industry employment size. The exposure measure used is based on a 1974 survey done by NIOSH, which gathered rough counts of worker exposure to different substances. The survey did not consider the intensity of the exposures, so it may not properly measure relative hazards across industries. Nonetheless, it is used by OSHA to target health inspections towards hazardous industries because better measures are not available. Its main disadvantage for our purposes is that no examination of changes in health hazards over time is possible.

The National Emissions Data System (NEDS) is used by EPA to keep track of air pollution emissions from almost 50,000 large, stationary point sources, of which 29,083 are manufacturing establishments. The universe of these plants is virtually identical with that of the EPA's Compliance Data System. The data set is based on records for each emission point within an establishment, although a record for total emissions from the establishment is also present. These records identify the SIC code for each establishment. The information for each point (and the total for the establishment) includes values for the emissions of five basic pollutants (particulates, carbon monoxide, hydrocarbons, sulfur dioxide, and nitrogen oxides) and the estimated efficiency of whatever emission control equipment is used for each pollutant. The emissions data may come from engineering estimates or actual measurements and have generally been updated at some point between 1973 and 1980.

Since the system contains no history of emissions, it is not possible to measure changes in emissions over time. The analysis in chapter 8 uses the mean annual particulate emissions for establishments with emissions data to measure relative pollution emitted by different industries. Particulates are analyzed because they are the most commonly emitted pollutant; still, only 339 industries have establishments with this emissions data present. The control equipment efficiency data, which could in principle be used to measure the extent of pollution cleanup in each industry, are not in good enough condition to make comparisons across industries meaningful. The limited scope of the NEDS data is troublesome, but there is no alternative emissions data available on an industry basis.

6.6. Summary

A large number of data sources have been assembled here to permit analysis of the impact of OSHA and EPA regulation on productivity. None of them are without problems, many related to changing SIC industry definitions over time, but others related simply to data of dubious quality or data which doesn't measure exactly the concept desired. Such problems affect all economic data sets, although they are more serious for some of these data sets than usual. Despite the data quality problems, there are no substitutes available of higher quality.

7

Regulation's Impact on Productivity: Empirical Analysis

7.1. Introduction

This chapter presents the results of an empirical analysis of the impact of OSHA and EPA regulation on productivity. The data show a slowdown in average industry productivity growth during the 1970s similar to the slowdown seen previously in the aggregate data. Differences across industries in the amount of OSHA and EPA regulation faced are shown to be positively correlated with differences in the magnitude of the productivity slowdown. This result is not sensitive to the particular form of the model or to the estimating procedure. It is also unaffected by the inclusion of alternative explanations for the slowdown. Extensions of the model along various dimensions are presented, giving more information about the link between regulation and productivity without changing the estimates of its magnitude.

7.2. Productivity Slowdown

Before attempting to explain the slowdown in productivity growth, one should be certain that the data used here show a productivity slowdown, and that they generally agree with the aggregate productivity statistics discussed earlier. The average industry growth rates for both labor and total factor productivity growth are presented in table 7.1 and figure 7.1. The labor productivity growth rates are obtained for each industry by subtracting the growth rate of worker hours from the growth rate of output (real industry shipments). Total factor productivity is calculated as the growth rate of output minus the growth rates of five inputs (nonproduction worker hours, production worker hours, nonenergy materials, energy, and real depreciated capital stock), with each input's growth rate weighted by its share in total cost.[1]

The first part of table 7.1 shows that there was a slowdown in average industry productivity growth during the 1970s. The average industry growth rate of labor productivity fell from 2.9 percent per year in 1958–69 to 0.9 percent per year in 1973–80, similar to the drop in labor productivity growth, as measured by the BLS, from 3.0 percent to 1.3 percent across these periods. Total factor productivity growth rates also fell during this period, as they did in the studies previously cited. For closer comparison with the aggregate numbers from other sources, growth rates weighted by industry size (value of shipments for total factor productivity and worker hours for labor productivity) are also included in the table and are presented in figure 7.1. The slowdown is similar in magnitude and timing to that described in chapter 5. The highly cyclical nature of productivity fluctuations is again apparent in figure 7.1. We turn now to an examination of the determinants of this slowdown.

7.3. Simple Regulation: Productivity Relationship

We have two measures of productivity growth: labor productivity and total factor productivity. To reduce the impact of strong cyclical fluctuations in productivity on the analysis, the average annual productivity growth rate for each industry is calculated for the periods 1959–69 and 1973–78. The analysis seeks to explain differences across industries in productivity growth rates in the latter period, and differences in the slowdown in productivity growth between the former and latter periods. The periods were chosen to match the cycle of productivity fluctuations from peak to peak, averaging out the impact on productivity of single years with cyclically high or low demand.[2] The earlier period was chosen to end before the regulatory agencies studied here began operating, to ensure that the measures of levels of regulation in the later period would also measure changes in regulation from the earlier period.

For measures of regulation we have the OSHA inspection rate per establishment and per employee, capital expenditures for employee safety and health as a share of the industry's capital stock, pollution abatement capital expenditures as a share of the industry's capital stock, pollution abatement operating costs as a share of the industry's materials cost, and the EPA establishment inspection rate. The analysis uses the average of each regulation measure over the 1974 to 1978 period.[3]

Table 7.2 presents means and standard deviations of these variables, as well as a correlation matrix. Several things can be learned from the correlations. First, all of the productivity measures are strongly positively correlated. Second, all of the regulation measures (except safety and health investment) are negatively correlated with all of the productivity measures.

Figure 7.1. Weighted Industry Productivity, 1961–80

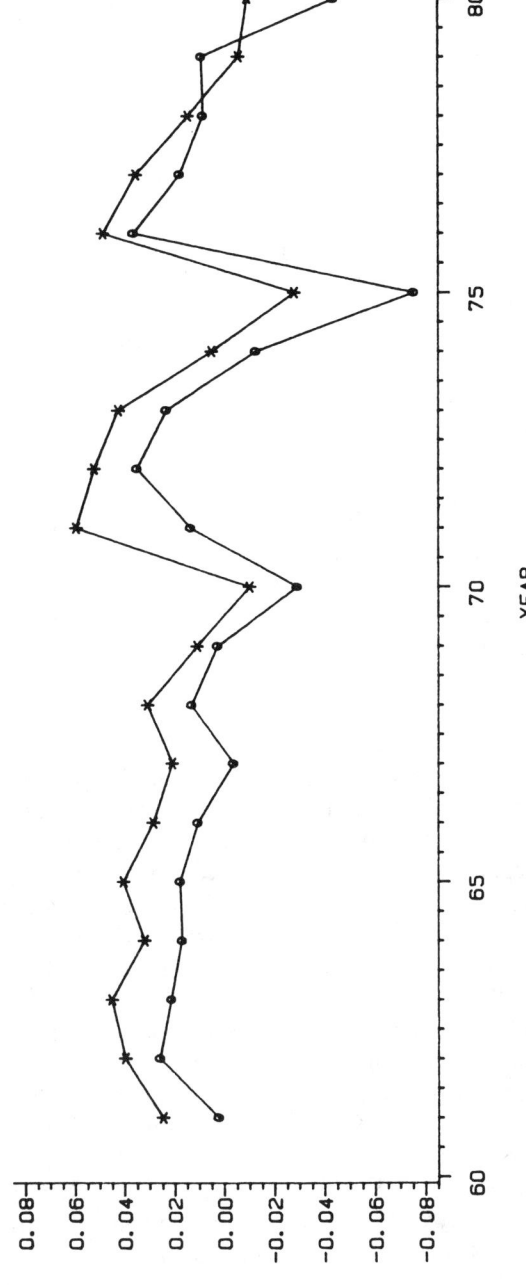

* = Labor Productivity   o = Total Factor Productivity

Table 7.1. Average Industry Productivity Growth Rates

Period:	1958-80	1958-69	1969-73	1973-78	1973-80
Industry Average					
Labor	2.37	2.88	3.62	1.48	0.87
Total Factor	0.44	0.96	0.95	-0.54	-0.67
Weighted Industry Average[1]					
Labor	2.44	3.03	3.60	1.50	0.86
Total Factor	0.49	1.15	1.06	-0.52	-0.86

1. Labor productivity averages are weighted by total employee hours.
   Total factor productivity averages are weighted by value of shipments.

Finally, all of the regulation measures (again except for safety and health investment) are positively correlated with each other.

The safety and health investment variable appears to be a poor measure of compliance costs associated with OSHA regulation, not especially surprising given its limitations mentioned in chapter 6. Although the variable was tested in other parts of the analysis, the results are not reported and were never significant.

The regression results found in table 7.3 show the connection between total factor productivity growth and the measures of regulation.[4] Each measure of regulation has a significant negative impact on each of the productivity measures when the regulation measures are considered independently. When the regulation measures are entered in pairs (one OSHA and one EPA) the coefficients for both measures fall. This is reasonable given the positive correlations between types of regulation noted above. The coefficients, however, generally remain significant. The results for OSHA establishment rates and pollution abatement capital expenditures are not shown here. They are similar to the results for OSHA employee inspection rates and pollution abatement operating costs, respectively.

Given this evidence for a regulation-productivity link, can we tell how important it is quantitatively? The R^2s from the regressions indicate what fraction of the variation in productivity growth across industries can be explained by the regulation measures. They tend to be small, indicating that, even using the "best" model, only about 4-5 percent of productivity growth variation is explained. This is due in large measure to the calculation of

Table 7.2. Descriptive Statistics

```
Index-Name                Description

 1 TFPCHG      Change in annual TFP growth rate: 1959-69 to 1973-78
 2 TFP7378     Annual TFP growth rate 1973-78
 3 LPCHG       Change in annual LP growth rate: 1959-69 to 1973-78
 4 LP7378      Annual LP growth rate 1973-78
 5 OSHINS      OSHA employee inspection rate 1974-78
 6 OSHEST      OSHA establishment inspection rate 1974-78
 7 EPAINS      EPA establishment inspection rate 1974-78
 8 PACE        Pollution abatement capital expenditures
              as share of real capital stock, 1974-78
 9 PAOC        Pollution abatement operating costs
              as share of materials cost, 1974-78
10 SAFINV      Employee safety and health investment
              as share of real capital stock, 1974-78
```

Index	Name	Mean (s.d)
1	TFPCHG	-.0146(.032)
2	TFP7378	-.0054(.029)
3	LPCHG	-.0130(.037)
4	LP7378	.0148(.034)
5	OSHINS	.5404(.665)
6	OSHEST	.1908(.212)
7	EPAINS	.0441(.114)
8	PACE	.0041(.007)
9	PAOC	.0056(.009)
10	SAFINV	.0026(.001)

Number of observations   450

Correlations

	1	2	3	4	5	6	7	8	9	10
1	1.0	.86	.76	.66	-.14	-.12	-.12	-.11	-.18	.14
2	.86	1.0	.67	.76	-.16	-.16	-.17	-.15	-.21	.12
3	.76	.67	1.0	.85	-.22	-.23	-.18	-.18	-.16	.14
4	.66	.76	.85	1.0	-.20	-.20	-.11	-.13	-.10	.14
5	-.14	-.16	-.22	-.20	1.0	.71	.37	.45	.27	-.13
6	-.12	-.16	-.23	-.20	.71	1.0	.57	.65	.42	-.11
7	-.12	-.17	-.18	-.11	.37	.57	1.0	.64	.62	.03
8	-.11	-.15	-.18	-.13	.45	.65	.64	1.0	.64	.10
9	-.18	-.21	-.16	-.10	.27	.42	.62	.64	1.0	.01
10	.14	.12	.14	.14	-.13	-.11	.03	.10	.01	1.0

Table 7.3. Initial Regression Results

(Basic Data Set, N = 450)
(standard errors in parentheses)

Dep.Var.	Mean	Model	Const.	OSHINS	EPAINS	PAOC	R^2(SSE)
TFPCHG	-.0146	A1	-.0110 (.0019)	-.0068 (.002)	-	-	.020 (.445)
		A2	-.0132 (.0016)	-	-.033 (.013)	-	.014 (.447)
		A3	-.0109 (.0018)	-	-	-.659 (.17)	.032 (.440)
		A4	-.0108 (.0019)	-.0055 (.002)	-.021 (.014)	-	.025 (.442)
		A5	-.0089 (.0020)	-.0048 (.002)	-	-.556 (.18)	.041 (.435)
TFP7378	-.0054	B1	-.0015 (.0018)	-.0072 (.002)	-	-	.027 (.374)
		B2	-.0035 (.0015)	-	-.043 (.012)	-	.028 (.373)
		B3	-.0015 (.0016)	-	-	-.701 (.16)	.042 (.368)
		B4	-.0012 (.0017)	-.0052 (.002)	-.031 (.013)	-	.040 (.369)
		B5	.0007 (.0018)	-.0051 (.002)	-	-.591 (.16)	.055 (.363)

Fraction of Total Drop in Productivity Growth
Attributed to Regulatory Variables

Model	All-Reg	OSHINS	EPAINS	PAOC
A1	.25	.25	-	-
A2	.10	-	.10	-
A3	.25	-	-	.25
A4	.26	.20	.06	-
A5	.39	.18	-	.21

For each of the TFPCHG equations the constant term measures the estimated change in productivity growth if regulation had been zero. The mean of the dependent variable is the actual change in productivity growth. The difference between these two numbers is the estimated contribution of regulation to productivity growth (negative in all cases). This is expressed above as a fraction of the actual productivity decline.

productivity as a residual: input growth accounts for most of the variation in output growth rates, so much of the remaining variation in output growth is due to random disturbances.[5]

The significant coefficients on the regulation measures in the regressions indicate that regulation is related to productivity growth. What is needed is a way to predict what productivity growth would have been in the absence of regulation. Consider again equation 4.1: measured productivity growth is actual productivity growth minus the effect of inputs used for compliance. In the absence of regulation (when all regulatory measures would be zero) the predicted mean productivity growth rate would be the constant term from the regression. The difference between this no-regulation productivity growth and the actual productivity growth is the estimated impact of regulation on productivity growth.

Table 7.3 presents this impact as a fraction of the observed productivity decline for each of the productivity change equations. From equation A5 (the productivity equation with the best fit), we estimate that regulation was responsible for slowing annual productivity growth by 0.57 percent. This represents 39 percent of the average industry slowdown in productivity growth (1.46 percent), due in roughly equal measure to OSHA and EPA regulation.[6] The next section examines some possible problems with this analysis and considers alternative explanations of the productivity slowdown.

7.4. Possible Objections

Although the results of the previous section suggest that regulation has had a significant impact on productivity, we should consider some possible objections to these results. There are (at least) four major lines of attack on the results presented above. First, there could be a problem with the measurement of productivity or regulation. Second, the linear regression model might be giving excessive weight to a few outlying industries with high regulation and poor productivity performance. Third, there could be some other explanation for the slowdown, omitted here, that happens to coincide with the regulatory measures. Finally, the regulation itself might be endogenous to the model, a possibility which is not addressed here but which could provide an important topic for future research.

7.4.1. Measurement Problems

Concerning the measurement problem, it is often argued that productivity indexes contain substantial measurement errors, especially due to the need to deflate output and some inputs, using imperfect price indexes. Unless these measurement errors are correlated with the regulation measures, they should not affect the estimated impact of regulation. Similarly, errors in the measurement of regulation will tend to bias the estimated coefficients on regulation towards zero. Neither source of measurement error seems a likely explanation of the results.

Allocation of missing values for pollution abatement operating cost might create a measurement problem. Since these allocated values tend to be small, dropping all industries with average annual pollution abatement operating cost less than $1 million eliminates most of the industries with allocated values. This also removes the textile industries which had been assigned PAOC values of zero.[7] When this correction is made, the basic results are not affected (see table 7.4).

7.4.2. Outliers and Non-Linearity

Linear regression results may be greatly affected by the values for a few outlying observations when the majority of the observations lie close together. In these data, there are a few industries with very high regulation values.[8] If these industries had very poor productivity performance they could by themselves produce large, negative coefficients on the regulation variables. Two procedures for dealing with this are considered: first, eliminate the outliers and repeat the regressions; second, use alternative estimation methods not so dependent on outlying values.

Table 7.4 presents results obtained when a few industries with exceptionally high regulation values are excluded from the regression. The coefficients on PAOC are almost identical to those found earlier. The coefficients on OSHINS are nearly twice as large as those found earlier. This could be due to the influence of the outlying industries, showing less additional impact from regulation at high regulation levels. This non-linearity is also tested for in table 7.4 by including squared and interacted regulation variables in the regression on the complete data set. No significant non-linearity is found and the average impact of regulation on productivity is not greatly affected, but there is an indication that the marginal impact of OSHINS falls for industries with very high OSHINS values. Deleting industries with small dollar values for PAOC (which might be poorly measured) does not noticeably change the results.

In table 7.5 we see two alternative tests of the connection between regulation and productivity. The first test separates the data set into quartiles, based on the value for each of the regulation variables. The average productivity growth rate and change in growth rates are presented for each quartile. In every case, both productivity growth rates and changes in productivity growth rates fall as regulation rises across quartiles. This

Table 7.4. Outlier and Non-Linearity Analysis

Regressions on Subsets Excluding Outliers
(standard errors in parentheses)

Subset:	Exclude High OSHINS, PAOC[1]			Also Exclude Low PAOC[2]		
	Mean	TFPCHG	TFP7378	Mean	TFPCHG	TFP7378
OSHINS	.475 (.45)	-.0094 (.004)	-.0085 (.003)	.550 (.48)	-.0091 (.004)	-.0083 (.003)
PAOC	.0050 (.007)	-.5826 (.228)	-.6578 (.208)	.0064 (.008)	-.5345 (.234)	-.6443 (.209)
constant		-.0069 (.0023)	.0023 (.0021)		-.0076 (.0028)	.0022 (.0025)
mean dep var		-.0143 (.032)	-.0050 (.029)		-.0160 (.031)	-.0065 (.028)
R^2 (SSE)		.045 (.428)	.054 (.357)		.047 (.284)	.066 (.226)
N		438	438		304	304

1. Excludes 7 industries with OSHINS > 3.0 and 5 with PAOC > .04.
2. Excludes 134 additional industries with 1974-78 average pollution abatement operating costs < $1M.

Basic Model: Non-linearity Test
(standard errors in parentheses)

Dep Var	Constant	OSHINS	PAOC	OSH*PAOC	OSH*OSH	PAOC*PAOC	R^2(SSE)
TFPCHG	-.0044	-.0150 (.005)	-.980 (.522)	.092 (.211)	.0026 (.0014)	10.03 (11.3)	.054 (.429)
TFP7378	.0032	-.0098 (.005)	-.950 (.479)	.014 (.194)	.0013 (.0013)	9.34 (10.4)	.060 (.361)

confirms that the earlier results are not due solely to the presence of a few industries with high regulation and poor productivity performance.

The Spearman rank correlation measure shown in table 7.5 provides a test for the connection between regulation and productivity that is not sensitive to outlying values. The results from this test indicate the same negative correlations between regulation and productivity that were found in table 7.2 for Pearson correlations. All of these correlations are significant. These analyses support the conclusion that the results presented earlier, which showed a significant relation between regulation and productivity growth, are not the result of a few outliers or the limitations of the linear regression model.

76 *Impact on Productivity: Empirical Analysis*

Table 7.5. Non-Parametric Analysis

Mean TFP by Regulation Quartiles

Name	Quartile	Mean	TFPCHG	TFP7378
OSHINS	1	.122	-.0072	.0009
	2	.256	-.0087	.0002
	3	.461	-.0204	-.0104
	4	1.325	-.0223	-.0125
EPAINS	1	.0003	-.0085	.0004
	2	.0032	-.0126	-.0016
	3	.0123	-.0150	-.0064
	4	.1613	-.0225	-.0141
PAOC	1	.0008	-.0075	-.0003
	2	.0021	-.0126	-.0021
	3	.0038	-.0180	-.0074
	4	.0158	-.0205	-.0120

Spearman Rank Correlation Coefficients
(P-values in parentheses)

	TFPCHG	TFP7378	OSHINS	EPAINS	PAOC
TFPCHG	1.0	.81(.001)	-.19(.001)	-.13(.006)	-.17(.001)
TFP7378	.81(.001)	1.0	-.19(.001)	-.18(.001)	-.18(.001)
OSHINS	-.19(.001)	-.19(.001)	1.0	.46(.001)	.36(.001)
EPAINS	-.13(.006)	-.18(.001)	.46(.001)	1.0	.61(.001)
PAOC	-.17(.001)	-.18(.001)	.36(.001)	.61(.001)	1.0

7.4.3. *Omitted Alternative Explanations*

For the omission of an explanation for the slowdown to bias the estimated relationship between regulation and productivity, two things must be true. The missing factor must be correlated with differences in productivity growth across industries during this period. It must also be correlated with differences in the regulatory measures across industries. Most of the potential factors would seem to fail one or the other of these tests, but a prime candidate is the increase in energy prices. Energy-intensive industries tend to have high pollution control expenditures, especially for air pollution, and the increase in energy prices may have forced the retirement of a substantial fraction of the capital stock in these industries, contributing to the productivity slowdown.

Table 7.6 tests the importance of energy usage as an alternative explanation by including energy intensity (measured by the share of energy in total cost) in regressions of productivity growth on regulation variables.

Energy intensity has a significant negative effect on productivity growth rates and changes in productivity growth rates when regulation variables are not present in the model. However, when regulatory variables are added, with or without interacting regulation with energy intensity, the impact of energy intensity becomes insignificant. The estimated effect of the regulation variables on productivity growth is only slightly reduced by the presence of the energy intensity variable. This effect is concentrated on pollution regulation, as expected.

A possible decline in the productive efficiency of the measured capital stock is examined in the latter half of table 7.6. More capital-intensive industries do have slower productivity growth, but including capital intensity in the basic regressions reduces only slightly the estimated impact of regulation on productivity. The analysis presented in chapter 4 suggests that regulation might affect productivity through obsolescence of the capital stock, so part of the impact of capital intensity on productivity might be due to regulation. Other input cost shares were tested, but they had little or no impact on productivity growth rates and no impact on the estimated regulation coefficients (and are not reported here).

Two additional explanations are considered in table 7.7. The first is that the poor macroeconomic performance of the 1970s contributed to slower productivity growth by depressing output growth over the entire business cycle. Measuring this on an industry level is difficult, because measures of output and input growth already enter the calculations of the dependent variables. The measure used here is the change in the growth rate of production worker hours between the 1959–69 and the 1973–78 periods. Its coefficient is significant, with the expected positive sign (industries not cutting back on their use of production workers do not suffer as large a productivity slowdown), but its inclusion does not affect the regulation coefficients.

The second explanation is that, for some reason, regulation is applied most heavily to mature industries, which have declining productivity growth relative to other industries. The measure used is the change in productivity growth between the 1959–63 and the 1963–69 periods. It is significantly positively related to productivity growth during the 1970s, indicating that industries with rising productivity growth during the 1960s also did better in the 1970s. However, the measure is not significantly related to the productivity slowdown, and does not affect the regulation coefficients substantially. Entering both explanations together also has little effect on the regulation coefficients.

Another explanation which has been offered for the productivity slowdown is a decline in spending on research and development (R&D) or a decline in the efficacy of such spending, either of which is assumed to slow the development of improved production techniques. Disaggregated data from

Table 7.6. Energy Intensity and Capital Intensity

(Basic data set, N = 450)
(standard errors in parentheses)

Dep Var	Const.	OSHINS	PAOC	ENSH[1]	CAPSH[2]	R^2(SSE)
A1 TFPCHG	-.0112			-.212		.021
	(.0019)			(.07)		(.444)
A2 TFP7378	-.0016			-.233		.030
	(.0017)			(.06)		(.372)
B1 TFPCHG	-.0085	-.0049	-.439	-.066		.042
	(.0021)	(.0023)	(.24)	(.09)		(.435)
B2 TFP7378	.0012	-.0051	-.441	-.085		.057
	(.0019)	(.0021)	(.22)	(.09)		(.362)
C1 TFPCHG	.0011				-.060	.022
	(.0052)				(.02)	(.444)
C2 TFP7378	.0031				-.032	.007
	(.0048)				(.02)	(.381)
D1 TFPCHG	.0055	-.0057	-.452		-.055	.059
	(.0054)	(.0023)	(.18)		(.02)	(.427)
D2 TFP7378	.0074	-.0055	-.543		-.026	.059
	(.0049)	(.0021)	(.17)		(.02)	(.361)
E1 TFPCHG	.0056	-.0057	-.380	-.041	-.054	.059
	(.0054)	(.0023)	(.24)	(.09)	(.02)	(.427)
E2 TFP7378	.0075	-.0055	-.415	-.074	-.024	.061
	(.0049)	(.0021)	(.22)	(.09)	(.02)	(.361)

Fraction of TFP Drop Attributed to Regulation

Model	All-Reg	OSHINS	PAOC	Controlling For ENSH	Controlling For CAPSH
B	.35	.18	.17	X	
D	.38	.21	.17		X
E	.36	.21	.15	X	X

1. Energy cost share (in total cost), 1969–73, mean = .016, s.d. = .022.
2. Capital cost share (in total cost), 1969–73, mean = .263, s.d. = .078.

Scherer (1981) is used, taken from a cross-section data set for 193 manufacturing industries in 1974. Because the data measure differences in levels of R&D spending rather than changes in R&D spending, they can only be used to explain differences in productivity growth rates rather than changes in growth rates over time. The industry data, both productivity and regulation variables, were aggregated into 193 sectors to match the R&D data, and the

Table 7.7. Cyclical and Declining Industry Controls

(Basic data set, N = 450)
(standard errors in parentheses)

	Cons.	OSHINS	PAOC	GLPCHG[1]	TFPCHGX[2]	R^2 (SSE)
TFPCHG	-.0068	-.0049	-.570	.094		.066
	(.0021)	(.0023)	(.177)	(.027)		(.424)
TFP7378	.0018	-.0051	-.599	.052		.064
	(.0019)	(.0021)	(.163)	(.025)		(.360)
TFPCHG	-.0088	-.0050	-.547		-.024	.043
	(.0020)	(.0023)	(.179)		(.028)	(.435)
TFP7378	.0003	-.0044	-.635		.118	.098
	(.002)	(.0021)	(.160)		(.025)	(.346)
TFPCHG	-.0067	-.0050	-.563	.093	-.018	.067
	(.0021)	(.0023)	(.177)	(.028)	(.028)	(.424)
TFP7378	.0016	-.0044	-.645	.060	.122	.110
	(.0019)	(.0021)	(.159)	(.025)	(.025)	(.342)

1. Change in growth rate of production workers between 1959-69 period and 1973-78 period.
2. Change in TFP growth rate between 1959-63 period and 1963-69 period.

basic analyses from section 7.3 were redone for this data set. The results obtained are similar to those found for the basic data set, as equation (1) in table 7.8 indicates.

Table 7.8 presents the results of regressions of productivity growth rates on R&D spending levels, with and without measures of regulation present. As expected, industries with higher R&D spending have higher levels of productivity growth. This result is not affected by the addition of the regulation variables. One interesting result is shown in equations (6) and (7), which indicate that the negative impact of regulation on productivity is concentrated in industries with high R&D spending.[9] The estimated effect of the regulation measures evaluated at the mean R&D level is not greatly affected. Without data on changes in R&D spending for each industry, which would permit analysis of changes in productivity growth rates, we cannot draw firm conclusions about the contribution of R&D spending to the productivity slowdown.

Table 7.8. Analysis Including R&D Data

Descriptive Statistics
(N = 193)

Correlations

Var	Mean	s.d.	TFP7378	OSHINS	PAOC	R+D-ORIG[1]	R+D-USE[2]
TFP7378	-.0099	.026	1.0	-.19	-.20	.24	.20
OSHINS	.6681	.699	-.19	1.0	.25	.01	.01
PAOC	.0065	.010	-.20	.25	1.0	.01	.22
R+D-ORIG[1]	.0331	.038	.24	.01	.01	1.0	.58
R+D-USE[2]	.0134	.015	.20	.01	.22	.58	1.0

Regression Results
(standard errors in parentheses)
Dependent variable = TFP7378

Var	(1)	(2)	(3)	(4)	(5)	(6)	(7)
Const.	-.0034	-.0154	-.0145	-.0088	-.0085	-.0149	-.0133
OSHINS	-.0055	-	-	-.0056	-.0051	-.0001	-.0012
	(.0027)			(.0026)	(.0026)	(.0031)	(.0042)
PAOC	-.431	-	-	-.434	-.582	.015	-.191
	(.19)			(.18)	(.19)	(.23)	(.29)
R+DORIG[1]	-	.164	-	.166	-	.453	-
		(.048)		(.047)		(.073)	
R+DUSE[2]	-	-	.344	-	.433	-	.922
			(.12)		(.12)		(.236)
OSH*R+D[3]	-	-	-	-	-	-.296	-.487
						(.086)	(.352)
PAOC*R+D[4]	-	-	-	-	-	-15.3	-20.94
						(5.16)	(12.9)
R^2	.063	.058	.039	.122	.122	.227	.155
SSE	.120	.120	.123	.112	.112	.099	.108

1. R&DORIG is R&D spending done by the sector, divided by capital stock.
2. R&DUSE is R&D spending used by the sector, divided by capital stock.
3. OSH*R&D is the interaction of OSHINS and the R&D measure used in that regression.
4. PAOC*R&D is the interaction of PAOC and the R&D measure used in that regression.

7.5. Extensions and Tests

7.5.1. Comparisons with Predicted Results

In chapter 4 we saw that productivity measures should be corrected if some inputs were used for compliance with regulations rather than for producing output. Equation 4.1 showed that the fractions of each input used for compliance purposes should be added together, each weighted by that input's share in total cost. There are two problems with applying this equation to the present data. First, for OSHA regulation we have no useable compliance cost measures, only enforcement measures. Second, the EPA compliance cost measure used most often (operating costs) does not refer to a single input, so it is difficult to know which cost share to use in weighting.[10] Table 7.9 presents the results of some experimentation with the data.

Pollution abatement capital spending should be weighted by capital's cost share in order to adjust input growth for compliance inputs. The mismeasured input effect would suggest a coefficient of -1.0 in a regression of productivity growth on capital's cost share times pollution abatement capital divided by total capital. In fact, the coefficient is -3.62. This is not necessarily inconsistent with the mismeasured input effect, because the larger coefficient could represent the impact of other compliance costs, such as pollution abatement operating costs or OSHA compliance costs, that are positively correlated with pollution abatement capital costs but not included in this regression. However, many reasons exist for regulation's impact on productivity to exceed the mismeasured input effect, some of them presented in chapter 4.[11]

How should one interpret the results presented in table 7.9? The relation between pollution abatement capital and productivity is less strong when the regulation measure is weighted by cost shares of inputs other than capital. Both the mismeasured input effect and other models of regulation's impact on productivity predict that the same percentage usage of an input for compliance purposes will matter more to an industry which makes relatively heavy use of that input. Here, industries which are more capital-intensive are more affected by the fraction of capital used for pollution abatement.

In fact, all of the regulation variables are strongest when weighted by capital's cost share. Although not as obviously expected for the other variables as it was for pollution abatement capital, this is consistent with two observations about regulation presented in chapter 3. First, much of the cost of complying with regulation comes in changes in capital stock required by the regulation. Second, the adjustment to regulation will be harder for industries with capital-intensive production, since they have relatively more fixed inputs, which are difficult to adjust.

Table 7.9. Impact of Weighted Regulation Measures

(weighted by input cost shares)
(Basic Data Set, N = 450)
(standard errors in parentheses)
Dependent variable = TFPCHG

Regulation Measure	Unweighted	Weighted by Input Cost Shares				
		NPL	PL	MAT	EN	CAP
Pollution capital						
Coefficient	-.468	-13.66	-4.20	-.405	-12.29	-3.62
	(.199)	(4.55)	(1.62)	(.288)	(3.97)	(.966)
R^2	.012	.020	.015	.004	.021	.031
(SSE)	(.448)	(.445)	(.447)	(.452)	(.444)	(.440)
Pollution operating cost						
Coefficient	-.659	-8.79	-2.79	-1.41	-5.73	-2.03
	(.172)	(2.76)	(1.01)	(.386)	(2.15)	(.526)
R^2	.032	.026	.017	.029	.016	.032
	(.440)	(.442)	(.446)	(.441)	(.447)	(.439)
EPA inspections						
Coefficient	-.033	-.941	-.281	-.039	-.414	-.145
	(.013)	(.294)	(.104)	(.024)	(.174)	(.045)
R^2	.014	.022	.016	.006	.013	.023
(SSE)	(.447)	(.444)	(.447)	(.451)	(.448)	(.443)
OSHA inspections						
Coefficient	-.0068	-.075	-.028	-.0084	-.175	-.039
	(.0022)	(.028)	(.011)	(.0038)	(.053)	(.010)
R^2	.020	.016	.014	.011	.024	.033
(SSE)	(.445)	(.447)	(.448)	(.449)	(.443)	(.439)

Note on interpretation: Since the coefficients on the weighted regulation measures tend to vary inversely with the magnitude of the weights, one should look at R^2 or SSE to see which weighted value is most strongly correlated with the productivity slowdown.

The results suggest that regulation has had a larger impact on productivity than would have been predicted by the available compliance cost measures, considering only the mismeasured input effect. Also, regulation has had a greater impact on productivity in more capital-intensive industries. Both of these conclusions were suggested by the analysis of chapter 4, and provide support for the research strategy followed here of estimating, rather than simply calculating, the impact of regulation on productivity.

7.5.2. Other Impacts of Regulation

This study concentrates on the impact of regulation on productivity. However, there are many other dimensions of production that could be affected by regulation. A wide variety of possible effects is examined in table 7.10, and some of them are discussed below.

Both levels of and changes in output growth rates are negatively related to regulation, although this effect is significant only for OHSA regulation. Input growth rates are not significantly affected by regulation, except for energy use which grew more (declined less) in more regulated industries. Regulation did not seem to lead to greater use of nonproduction workers, either in absolute terms or relative to production workers. This is a surprise if one pictures much of the cost of regulation coming in the form of greater paperwork for firms, or more managers needed to cope with regulatory constraints.

Only a crude measure of profitability is available. This is revenues accruing to capital (the residual after other inputs' payments are subtracted from the value of shipments) divided by the capital stock. As one might expect, industries which are more heavily regulated have significantly lower profitability. However, there is no significant relationship between regulation and changes in profitability. Therefore, the more regulated industries had lower profitability during the 1960s as well as during the 1970s. This result differs from the productivity results presented earlier, where both levels of and changes in productivity growth rates were negatively correlated with regulation.

The cost share data present a mixed picture. Nonproduction labor's share is negatively related to both OSHA and EPA regulation, another unexpected result. Energy's share is positively related to EPA regulation and negatively related to OSHA regulation, while the opposite is true for capital's share. The shares of production labor and materials are not greatly affected by regulation.

This section gives some indication of various aspects of industries which might be related to regulation. No attempt is made to model the variables presented here in any systematic way, so the results can only be suggestive.

7.5.3. Testing Growth Accounting

The decision to use growth accounting methods to calculate productivity growth requires that certain assumptions be maintained. A comprehensive test of these assumptions is not presented here. However, some simple tests of the contributions of different inputs to output and how these contributions changed over time are presented.

Table 7.10. Other Impacts of Regulation

Dep. Var.	Const.	OSHINS	PAOC	R^2(SSE)
	Growth in real value of shipments			
GSHIP7378[1]	.019	-.0088	-.249	.016
	(.003)	(.0039)	(.301)	(1.24)
GSHIPCHG[2]	-.025	-.0097	-.329	.016
	(.004)	(.0045)	(.349)	(1.66)
	Profit rate = (shipments - noncapital costs)/capital stock			
PROF7378[1]	1.20	-.103	-21.23	.136
	(.034)	(.039)	(3.05)	(127)
PROFCHG[2]	.438	.037	-1.89	.006
	(.021)	(.024)	(1.89)	(48.2)
	Input growth rates			
GNPLCHG[2]	-.011	.0013	.151	.001
	(.004)	(.005)	(.37)	(1.88)
GPLCHG[2]	-.023	.0001	.145	.001
	(.003)	(.004)	(.304)	(1.26)
GMATCHG[2]	-.018	-.0087	.668	.009
	(.005)	(.005)	(.407)	(2.26)
GENCHG[2]	-.094	.0098	1.25	.046
	(.004)	(.0046)	(.365)	(1.81)
GCAPCHG[2]	-.011	-.0021	.391	.008
	(.002)	(.0028)	(.215)	(.631)
	Factor shares			
SHNPLCHG[2]	-.034	-.038	-2.74	.041
	(.012)	(.014)	(1.07)	(15.6)
SHPLCHG[2]	-.135	-.012	-1.37	.011
	(.010)	(.011)	(.85)	(9.78)
SHMATCHG[2]	-.007	.014	.001	.008
	(.007)	(.079)	(.62)	(5.17)
SHENCHG[2]	.262	-.051	7.26	.059
	(.016)	(.018)	(1.43)	(27.8)
SHCAPCHG[2]	.102	.020	-3.40	.030
	(.010)	(.012)	(.93)	(11.8)

1. "7378" indicates average for 1973–78 period.
2. "CHG" indicates change between 1959–69 and 1973–78 periods.

Table 7.11. Cross-Industry "Production Function" Models

(Basic Data Set, N = 450)
(standard errors in parentheses)

	GSHIP5969		GSHIP7378		GSHIPCHG	
	(1)	(2)	(3)	(4)	(5)	(6)
Const.	.0102	.0068	.0019	-.0066	-.0113	-.0139
	(.0012)	(.0011)	(.0020)	(.0015)	(.0018)	(.0016)
WINPUT		1.069		1.064		1.045
		(.023)		(.033)		(.030)
WNPL	1.18		1.38		1.77	
	(.19)		(.20)		(.32)	
WPL	1.62		2.24		1.47	
	(.27)		(.30)		(.21)	
WMAT	1.12		1.00		.95	
	(.05)		(.06)		(.06)	
WEN	2.51		.80		2.60	
	(.60)		(.85)		(.84)	
WCAP	.42		.15		.07	
	(.08)		(.15)		(.15)	
R^2	.854	.830	.729	.697	.762	.733
SSE	.098	.114	.340	.381	.403	.452

Impact of Regulation

Dep. Var.		Input Growth Controls	OSHINS	PAOC	R^2(SSE)
GSHIP7378	(3)	5 separate inputs	-.0059	-.393	.741
			(.0020)	(.164)	(.326)
GSHIP7378	(4)	1 aggregate input	-.0049	-.614	.714
			(.0021)	(.163)	(.360)
GSHIPCHG	(5)	5 separate inputs	-.0055	-.395	.769
			(.0022)	(.188)	(.390)
GSHIPCHG	(6)	1 aggregate input	-.0046	-.566	.744
			(.0023)	(.179)	(.433)

Note: GSHIP is average annual growth rate of shipments. WINPUT is weighted sum of average input growth rates. All input growth rates are weighted by input cost shares.

86 *Impact on Productivity: Empirical Analysis*

The productivity growth calculations assumed that the contribution of each input's growth to output growth is given by that input's cost share. Thus, in a regression of industry output growth rates on input growth rates weighted by the inputs' respective cost shares, one would expect to find a coefficient of 1.0 on each weighted input growth measure. Results for these regressions are presented in table 7.11 for two periods, 1959 to 1969 and 1973 to 1978, and the change between them.

The clearest conclusion from this analysis is that capital growth was not related to output growth in the manner predicted by the growth accounting model. It contributed less than half the expected amount to output growth in the 1960s, and its contribution fell to near zero for the 1970s. This helps explain the earlier results that capital-intensive industries did poorly in the 1970s. A major reason for the decline in capital's contribution was probably the rapid obsolescence of existing capital due to regulation and higher energy prices. Inflation could also have caused problems with the measurement of capital input growth. Finally, the long recession in the 1970s led to low capital utilization rates, and unused capital does not contribute to output. Of course, these results could simply reflect serious problems in the measurement of capital growth rates.

The contributions of other inputs to output growth tend to exceed those predicted by growth accounting. Part of this arises from the low contribution of capital, since with constant returns to scale we would see the average of all coefficients at 1.0. In fact, when output growth is regressed on the average of all input growth rates (models 2, 4, and 6), the resulting coefficient is slightly above one and consistent over time. This suggests that output growth is more than proportional to input growth, and could indicate some increasing returns to scale.

The R^2s of these regressions are high, indicating that 70 percent or more of output growth can be explained by input growth. The productivity measure used in the earlier analysis excludes most of this predictable output growth, and its residual nature makes it much harder to achieve R^2s of any size. If regulation measures are added to these regressions explaining output growth rates (also shown in table 7.11), their coefficients are significant and almost identical to those found in the earlier productivity analysis.

It is important to recall that the regressions just presented do not constitute production function estimation in the usual sense. Each observation comes from a different industry, and one would not expect all of the industries to share a common production function. Also, the regression does not explicitly include a productivity term, although the constant term comes close, since it captures the average growth in output unexplained by input growth. There is some support for the growth accounting model: no coefficients are negative and most are around one. Still, this support is certainly not complete confirmation of the growth accounting assumptions, and the problems with measuring the contribution of capital are troubling.

7.6. Panel Data Analysis

Another way of examining the relationship between regulation and productivity is to consider year-to-year changes in both variables. This yields a panel data set with 450 industry observations in each year. One can then calculate the impact of yearly changes in the regulation measures on changes in productivity growth rates. Results from this analysis are found in table 7.12.

The coefficient on pollution abatement operating costs is similar to that found before (although no longer significant), while the OSHA inspection rate coefficient is substantially reduced. This differential change in coefficients could be due to the nature of the regulation variables. Operating cost measures resources used in each year. The OSHA inspection rate may be more representative of long-run compliance costs, to the extent that it measures costs. These long-run costs would not show up as clearly in an analysis of year-to-year changes.

The lack of significance for both variables may be attributable to the nature of the analysis. By ignoring all cross-industry variation in levels of regulation and concentrating on year-to-year changes, it depends on information more subject to measurement error. Still, there is some evidence for a relationship between changes in regulation and changes in productivity, though not as strong as that found before.

One can also use the panel data set presented here to extend the tests of the growth accounting model found in section 7.5.3. Instead of only one observation per industry there are several, one for each year. This permits the estimation of a different intercept term for each industry. The impact of weighted input growth on output growth is still constrained to be the same across industries.

The results from this analysis are presented in table 7.12. They are quite similar to the results from the simple cross-section analysis of section 7.5.3, with high R^2s and all inputs (except for capital) contributing significantly to output growth. As before, the coefficients on noncapital inputs are usually above one, offsetting the insignificant impact of capital. The coefficient on aggregate input growth is significantly larger than that found in the cross-section analysis. This is not surprising, because the annual fluctuations in industry input growth examined here are correlated with the cyclical factors influencing annual fluctuations in productivity growth. The major weakness of the growth accounting model is again seen to come in measuring the contribution of capital.

88 *Impact on Productivity: Empirical Analysis*

Table 7.12. Panel Data Analysis

(standard errors in parentheses)

Dep. Var.	Period	OSHINS	PAOC	R^2(SSE)	N
(1) TFP	1973-1980	-.0012 (.0022)	-.532 (.372)	.216 (19.1)	3150
(2) TFP	1973-1978	-.0019 (.0027)	-.512 (.455)	.250 (14.6)	2250

Cross-Industry 'Production Function' Models
Dependent Variable = GSHIP

	1959-1969		1973-1978	
	(1)	(2)	(3)	(4)
WINPUT		1.292 (.011)		1.285 (.021)
WNPL	.72 (.08)		1.37 (.15)	
WPL	2.00 (.06)		1.83 (.30)	
WMAT	1.23 (.02)		1.18 (.03)	
WEN	2.21 (.48)		1.54 (.27)	
WCAP	-.001 (.09)		.20 (.24)	
R^2 SSE	.820 (11.6)	.804 (12.7)	.789 (12.8)	.783 (13.2)
N	4500	4500	2250	2250

Note: Each regression contains 450 industry observations per year. TFP and GSHIP are the industry's growth rates for the year. Input growth rates (WNPL, WPL, WMAT, WEN, WCAP) are weighted by cost shares, and WINPUT is their sum. Regulation variables measure year-to-year changes, not levels. All regressions include 450 industry dummies and year dummies.

7.7. Long-Run Relationship

One final issue concerning the impact of regulation on productivity is the long-run relationship between regulation and productivity growth. Many of the possible connections between regulation and productivity mentioned in chapter 4 are temporary, lasting only until firms can adjust their use of fixed inputs. Perhaps the productivity slowdown of the 1970s represents a temporary cost of adjustment to a new business environment. In that case, continuation of regulation at the same level will not adversely affect future productivity. Alternatively, the increased level of regulation in the 1970s may permanently reduce future productivity growth.

Because the period when regulation data are available (1973–80) does not contain two complete business cycles, one cannot look at changes in average productivity growth across cycles as was done before. However, one can see whether those industries with high regulation values during the 1974–78 period continue to perform poorly in the 1978–80 period. This analysis is shown in table 7.13.

The levels of regulation during the 1974–78 period, which were significantly negatively correlated with productivity growth during that period, are not significantly correlated with later productivity growth rates. This suggests that the large impact of regulation on productivity estimated earlier may not be as great a concern in the long run, after the initial adjustment to the regulation has occurred.

7.8. Conclusions

The above analysis demonstrates a significant link between OSHA and EPA regulation and productivity growth, with highly regulated industries showing both lower productivity growth and a greater slowdown during the 1970s. The magnitude of this impact is larger than that found in earlier studies. The results also suggest that surveys of compliance costs may understate the cost to firms of regulation. Three qualifications to these results are important.

First, the analysis above equates levels of regulation in the 1970s with changes in regulation between the 1960s and the 1970s. This implicitly assumes that there was zero regulation in the 1960s. We did see in chapter 3 that the regulation introduced in the 1970s was much stronger than earlier regulation, having both higher standards and stricter enforcement, so the assumption of zero regulation in the 1960s may not be far wrong. However, to the extent that this assumption is false, the estimates of the contribution of regulation to the slowdown will be overstated.

Second, these results are based on data from a very turbulent period for the economy, with many factors other than regulation changing. Although several attempts were made to control for these other factors, without affecting the regulation results, not all other factors could be measured. Such omitted factors could bias the results.

Third, and most important, the results may reflect a temporary phenomenon rather than a permanent one. We saw in chapter 4 that many of the expected impacts of regulation on productivity are temporary ones. This is supported by the results presented in section 7 which found little or no long-run connections between regulation and productivity growth. Therefore, the

Impact on Productivity: Empirical Analysis

Table 7.13. Long-Run Impact of Regulation

(standard errors in parentheses)

Dep. Var.	Const.	OSHINS	PAOC	R^2(SSE)
TFP7880	-.010 (.003)	-.0022 (.0037)	.294 (.283)	.003 (1.09)

Note: The productivity variable is from the 1978-80 period, while the regulation measures are from the 1974-78 period.

estimates of relatively large productivity costs associated with regulation may reflect costs already paid, rather than costs that society will face in the future.

The next chapter examines the issue of regulatory enforcement in greater detail, looking for both targeting of enforcement towards problem industries and possible benefits from enforcement.

8
Benefits from Regulation

8.1. Introduction

Chapter 7 concentrated on the costs of OSHA and EPA regulation, measured in terms of foregone output. These costs are estimated to be quite large: if productivity growth in manufacturing is slowed by .5 percentage points per year between 1973 and 1978, manufacturing output in 1978 is 2.5 percent, or $13 billion, lower than it would otherwise have been. However, if one is trying to determine whether these regulations have helped or hurt society one must also consider the benefits which these regulations are supposed to provide in reducing environmental pollution and work-related injuries and illnesses. This chapter examines the available data for such benefits. Unfortunately, the data necessary for this are available only for work-related injuries.

We first review available information on the possible benefits from regulation. Then we examine the extent to which the regulatory agencies target their enforcement effort on industries which are performing poorly on measures of the goals of the agencies. Both OSHA and EPA enforcement efforts exhibit such targeting. Finally, estimates of the connection between OSHA safety inspections and industry injury rates are presented and compared with the results from previous studies.

8.2. Previous Estimates

Estimates of potential benefts from OSHA and EPA regulation are quite large, similar in magnitude to the estimates of the compliance costs presented earlier. Lave and Seskin (1977) estimate that complete compliance with EPA air pollution standards could reduce total deaths and illnesses by 7 percent, with a health benefit of $16.1 billion. Waddell (1974) estimates other benefits from cleaner air at $7.5 billion. In a comprehensive review of earlier studies, Freeman (1979) estimates that regulation of stationary source air pollution yielded benefits of $20.3 billion, based on previous studies of the costs of pollution and an assumed 20 percent reduction in emissions of particulates and sulfur oxides. He also calculates benefits from water pollution control (assuming best control technology in use) of $12.3 billion. Of course, these benefits are from pollution abatement throughout the economy, not just in manufacturing. If manufacturing was responsible for one-third of stationary source air pollution and one-fifth of water pollution, the potential benefit of regulation would be $9.2 billion.[1]

Occupational injuries and illnesses also impose substantial costs on society. Ashford (1976) presents evidence from the National Safety Council that occupational injuries cost $10 billion in 1971. More recent estimates cited in Green and Waitzman (1979) find even greater costs of occupational injuries, $23 billion in 1978, with a possible additional $10 billion if occupational illnesses are included. If we assume that manufacturing is responsible for about one-third of these costs, potential benefits from reducing workplace hazards would be $11 billion.[2] Eliminating all hazards is clearly not feasible, but in the interest of calculating potential (rather than actual) benefits, we come up with a total benefit from OSHA and EPA regulation of manufacturing totaling over $20 billion, which exceeds the rough cost estimate mentioned above, so there is the potential for a conclusion favorable to regulation. The question still remains: has regulation really reduced these problems, and if so, by how much?

The principal difficulty with trying to analyze the benefits of regulation is the scarcity of available data. To measure benefits, we need a measure of industry performance in a dimension addressed by regulation (such as air pollution emissions), and we need this measure for at least two dates, to see whether industry performance has improved or worsened and by how much. Inter-industry differences in the rates of improvement (positive or negative) can then be compared with differences in the measures of regulatory intensity used earlier. If heavily regulated industries have improved their performance relative to lightly regulated ones, we might view this as evidence of benefits from regulation.

Unfortunately, one of the assumptions used in the earlier analysis, that the regulation variables are exogenous to the other variables considered, is much less attractive when the other variables include a measure of industry performance. We might well expect OSHA to inspect high-hazard industries more frequently than low-hazard ones. Enforcement efforts by EPA are concentrated almost exclusively on plants with large amounts of emissions. Thus, positive correlations between enforcement effort and poor performance across industries could be due to the targeting of regulatory effort towards industries where the worst problems lie. The difficulty is most obvious when the level of performance (rather than the change in performance) is used, but it can also appear in analysis of changes. Suppose one relates changes in performance between the 1959–69 and 1973–78 periods to 1973–78 regulation (as was done for productivity performance). Unusually poor performance in the very early years of the latter period could lead to higher regulation later in that period. Care is needed in this case to avoid the conclusion that regulation leads to poor performance.

To do any tests at all we need measures of industry performance on worker safety, worker health and pollution emissions. The only one for which there are measures over time is worker safety, using industry injury rates. For pollution emissions there are the data from EPA's National Emissions Data System mentioned earlier, but that gives only one set of emissions data for each plant. For worker health there is an index of relative health hazards across industries, used by OSHA to help target their health inspections. This is also a single-point measure. Thus, the only area of regulation where one can test for benefits is OSHA regulation of worker safety, although one can examine all three areas for targeting of regulation towards industries with poor performance.

8.3. Targeting

Table 8.1 presents results which strongly suggest that regulation is targeted towards industries with poor performance. OSHA safety inspection rates are significantly higher in industries with high injury rates, and health inspection rates are significantly higher in industries with high health hazard levels. Each type of OSHA inspection rate is also related to the other performance index (based on analyses not presented here), but less strongly than to its own index, suggesting that there really is targeting at work. In fact, the OSHA national office mandates such targeting by the area offices.

The EPA inspection rates are positively correlated with a particulate emissions measure. Because of possible problems with this measure (related to differences across establishments in the date when the emissions variable was last updated), the EPA analysis is also done using air pollution operating costs, on the grounds that such abatement costs are positively correlated with emissions across industries. Over half of the inter-industry differences in EPA inspection rates are explained, mostly by differences in abatement expenditures.[3] In both cases, we find evidence that OSHA and EPA inspections are concentrated on industries with poor performance.

8.4. Benefits

If we believe that these inspections produce the benefits they are supposed to, we might conclude that the inspections are being allocated properly across industries, with more attention being paid to those industries which most need improvement. Unfortunately, table 8.2 provides no evidence of such benefits,

94 Benefits from Regulation

Table 8.1. Targeting of Enforcement Effort

Dep Var:	Mean(s.d)	SAFETY	HEALTH	EPAINS	EPAINS[6]
Const.		-.238 (.076)	-.074 (.028)	-.010 (.012)	.081 (.017)
UNION[1]	.458(.146)	.978 (.165)	.265 (.060)	.023 (.027)	.118 (.035)
ESTSIZE[2]	.099(.163)	.526 (.142)	.400 (.065)	.123 (.024)	.043 (.028)
INJ7478[3]	.512(.274)	.280 (.087)			
HAZINDEX[4]	.607(.472)		.099 (.019)		
PAOC	.0020(.0049)			15.34 (.80)	
EMITAVG[5]	.107(.289)				.033 (.017)
Dep var mean (s.d)		.405 (.511)	.149 (.178)	.044 (.114)	.146 (.094)
R^2		.166	.282	.513	.060
SSE		97.84	7.00	2.82	2.82
N		450	309	450	339

1. UNION is the fraction of production workers unionized, 1973–75.
2. ESTSIZE is the mean number of production workers per establishment, 1974–78.
3. INJ7478 is the mean lost workday injury rate, 1974–78.
4. HAZINDEX is the OSHA health hazard index (based on 1974 survey).
5. EMITAVG is the mean annual particulate emissions for establishments with emissions data (available for only 339 industries).
6. Here EPAINS is the mean inspection rate for establishments on the Compliance Data System (i.e., inspections/CDS establishments, not inspections/total establishments).

although the results may be due to the complicating influence of targeting on the analysis. The first regression considers the change in injury rates between the 1959–69 and 1974–78 periods. The significant positive relation between safety inspection rates and injury rates may well be due to the contemporaneous nature of injury and inspection rates during the 1974–78 period, as explained earlier. Changing the end-period to the year 1979, regression 2 also finds a positive inspection-injury relationship. Looking at changes in injury rates between 1972 and 1979 yields smaller, but still significant coefficients. Finally regressions 4 and 5 attempt to purge the

Table 8.2. Benefits from OSHA Safety Inspections

Dependent variable: changes in injury rates
(standard errors in parentheses)

	(1)	(2)	(3)	(4)	(5)
Time Period	59-69:73-78	59-69:79	72:79	72:79	72:79
Const.	-.036	.044	.279	.212	.186
	(0.42)	(.072)	(.051)	(.053)	(.054)
PRSHIP[1]	-.001	.130	.047	.026	.033
	(.083)	(.077)	(.075)	(.073)	(.075)
PRODEMP[2]	.103	.108	.195	.210	.217
	(.058)	(.052)	(.070)	(.068)	(.069)
PRCAP[3]	.035	-.029	-.0001	.043	.061
	(.072)	(.064)	(.075)	(.074)	(.076)
SAFETY	.236	.267	.113	.091	
	(.037)	(.039)	(.027)	(.027)	
SAFETYP[4]					.178
					(.076)
INJRAT Controls[5]				X	X
Dep var mean	.075	.259	.363	.363	.363
(s.d)	(.418)	(.442)	(.296)	(.296)	(.296)
R^2	.092	.124	.080	.152	.139
SSE	71.3	76.8	36.2	33.3	34.2

1. Percentage change in real value of shipments per production worker.
2. Percentage change in number of production workers.
3. Percentage change in real capital stock per production worker.
4. Predicted SAFETY from regression, table 8.1.
5. Regressions include 1976, 1977, and 1978 injury rates as controls.

inspection rate of its connection with injuries by including the industry's 1976, 1977, and 1978 injury rates in the regression and then replacing the inspection rate with its predicted value from the table 8.1 regression. There is still a significant and positive relation between inspection rates and changes in injury rates.

It seems quite difficult to use this data to demonstrate positive benefits of safety inspections on injury rates. This does not mean that such benefits are not there, although if the benefits were large one would have expected to observe some evidence of them. Previous studies examining the relationship between OSHA inspections and injury rates have yielded mixed results.

On the positive side, Bartel and Thomas (1982) and Cooke and Gautschi

96 *Benefits from Regulation*

(1981) both find a significant negative relationship between inspections and injury rates. Viscusi (1979b) and McCaffrey (1983) find no significant relation between inspections and injury rates. Mendeloff (1979) and Smith (1979) find beneficial results estimated for some versions of their models, no benefits from other versions.

In general, the studies which use data on individual plants tend to find benefits, while studies (such as this one) which use industry data are less likely to find benefits. When benefits are found, they are usually small: Bartel and Thomas find that a 10 percent change in inspection rates reduces injury rates by only .4 percent. Mendeloff concludes that relatively few injuries are caused by violations of OSHA standards, and most of these violations would not be detectable by an inspector. Therefore, the potential influence of OSHA safety inspections is limited.

8.5. Conclusions

This chapter has presented what little can be said about the benefits from regulation, given the data at hand. The results from the targeting analysis do suggest that enforcement effort is being directed towards those industries that are doing poorly at protecting their workers and the environment. However, the search for benefits from worker safety regulation was unsuccessful. It should be noted that the theoretical discussion from chapter 3 suggests that both worker health and pollution control offer a greater chance for benefits from regulation than is offered by worker safety regulation. Unfortunately, such benefits cannot be measured without better data.

9
Conclusions and Future Work

Although the completion of this study took a substantial amount of time and effort, it is in an important sense a preliminary study. The primary goal was to determine whether or not a connection existed between the productivity slowdown during the 1970s and the concurrent growth in federal regulation, especially through OSHA and EPA. A secondary goal was to provide an estimate of the magnitude of the connection and contrast it with previous estimates. Both of these tasks have been accomplished.

First, a connection between regulation and productivity is clearly shown by the data. Industries which faced a large amount of regulation experienced a larger than average productivity slowdown. This connection is not dependent on a few outlying industries, as the sensitivity analysis makes clear. This result does not seem to be the result of an omitted variable, since the inclusion of a variety of alternative explanations for the slowdown leaves the regulation coefficients essentially unchanged. Of course, one cannot hope to control for all possible omitted variables, but as more and more variables are tested without effect, one's confidence in the basic result increases. The results also remain when a more general "production function" model relating output and input growth replaces the total factor productivity measure.

In the process of establishing the connection between regulation and productivity, estimates of its magnitude are generated. These estimates seem quite high: a .57 percent contribution to the productivity slowdown, compared with Denison's largest estimate of .35 percent and many smaller estimates. There are three points that should be made regarding comparisons of the results presented here with others.

First, these results refer to the manufacturing sector, while many of the other estimates were based on economy-wide measures. Since manufacturing is more highly regulated than other sectors (with the notable exceptions of electric utilities and coal mining), a higher estimate here is not especially surprising. Estimates of EPA's impact on utilities are even higher than these. Also, manufacturing suffered less of a productivity slowdown than other

Conclusions

sectors, an important point when comparing percentages of the slowdown explained by regulation in different studies.

Second, the estimates presented here implicitly assume that regulation was zero during the 1960s, because they use measures of the level of regulation during the 1970s to measure the change in regulation between the 1960s and the 1970s. It is clear that regulation was much higher during the 1970s than it had been before (otherwise it wouldn't have been considered a likely candidate to explain the slowdown). It is also clear that there was some regulation earlier, before OSHA and EPA were created.

Consider how this affects the estimated impact of regulation. The calculation of a regulation variable's contribution to the slowdown is calculated by multiplying the mean of that variable (measured during the 1970s) times its regression coefficient. If the amount of new regulation is overstated, the variable mean will be too large. However, the variable coefficient will tend to be smaller than the true coefficient under these circumstances, which will offset the effect of the larger mean. The coefficient may also be affected if the distribution of the new regulation across industries was not simply a proportional increase above the old regulation. Neither of these effects is likely to affect the estimated impact of regulation on productivity, as long as the new regulation is several times as strong as the old regulation.

Third, many of the previous estimates of regulation's impact on productivity are calculations based on the growth accounting model and cost of compliance data. The results obtained here seem to be about twice as large as would be obtained using growth accounting. There are reasons why one would expect regulation to have a larger impact on productivity than growth accounting would indicate. These are described in some detail in chapter 4, but many are related to the need for businesses to adjust their production in the face of regulatory constraints. An implication of this would be that some of the impact of regulation on productivity should diminish over time as these adjustments are made. Some evidence supporting this is presented. Perhaps the long-run impact of regulation on productivity will be closer to the growth accounting estimates.

Some mention should be made of the analysis of benefits from regulation. The basic problem is the lack of available data on any level of industry detail. This is particularly true for measuring benefits from pollution abatement. There is substantial evidence that air pollution was reduced during the 1970s, almost certainly due to the existence of EPA regulation. However, this evidence is based on ambient air quality measures, with no way to link the improvement in air quality to reduced pollution from particular plants or industries.

More can be done with OSHA regulation, since injury data are observed for individual industries. That this study does not find benefits from the regulation does not preclude the existence of such benefits, and other studies have found some (small) benefits. It is important to recall that worker safety is the area where one would least expect to find benefits from regulation, due to the presence of compensating differentials and the difficulties of developing useful standards. Thus, the results of this study should not be read as a call for the dismantling of these regulations, especially since a large part of the costs of regulation, in terms of lower productivity growth, may represent a one-time adjustment cost, already paid during the 1970s.

Where do we go from here? Three possible areas on the research agenda should be mentioned: collecting more data, doing microeconomic analyses, and developing and estimating a more detailed model.

The collection of more data can proceed along two dimensions. As time passes, more years of data will become available. A few more years of data would provide the two complete business cycles needed to look properly at the impact of changes in regulation over time. Extending the data period would also allow more sophisticated use of the panel data. The other way to extend the data is through adding new variables. These could be measures of other explanations of the productivity slowdown, or they could be better measures of the benefits of regulation.

A different and more difficult process of data collection is needed to provide microeconomic data (on individual firms or establishments) which could be used to test for a connection between regulation and productivity at that level. The enforcement measures of regulation are available already on an establishment level. Compliance cost measures and productivity measures will be much more difficult to gather, although some researchers are beginning to put in the required effort. These case study analyses will be a valuable complement to the more aggregate numbers considered here.

Finally, more effort needs to be put into the underlying model connecting regulation and productivity. The results here indicate the connection, but a better understanding of how that connection operates is needed to see why higher regulation was associated with lower productivity, whether this connection is likely to continue, and what (if anything) can be done to reduce the harmful impact of regulation on productivity while maintaining or increasing the benefits that regulation was designed to provide.

Appendix

Distribution of Regulation Data

Table A.1. Regulation Measures: Top 10 Industries and Distributions

OSHINS - OSHA employee inspection rate

3332	Primary lead	5.95
3621	Motors and generators	4.27
3316	Cold finishing of steel shapes	4.21
3731	Ship building and repairing	4.19
3312	Blast furnaces and steel mills	4.02
3732	Boat building and repairing	3.94
3324	Steel investment foundries	3.50
2452	Prefabricated wood buildings	2.90
3511	Turbines and turbine generator sets	2.76
3671	Electron tubes, receiving type	2.71
	First quartile	.60
	Median	.33
	Third quartile	.19

EPAINS - EPA establishment inspection rate

3334	Primary aluminum	.912
3333	Primary zinc	.872
2951	Paving mixtures and blocks	.725
2061	Raw cane sugar	.644
3332	Primary lead	.636
2895	Carbon black	.621
2911	Petroleum refining	.597
3241	Cement, hydraulic	.493
3274	Lime	.492
3331	Primary copper	.482
	First quartile	.023
	Median	.006
	Third quartile	.001

PAOC - pollution abatement operating costs / materials cost

3241	Cement, hydraulic	.0585
2892	Explosives	.0557
3333	Primary zinc	.0516
2816	Inorganic pigments	.0491
2611	Pulp mills	.0474
3339	Primary nonferrous metals, nec	.0393
3296	Mineral wool	.0375
2646	Pressed and molded paper goods	.0373
2631	Paperboard mills	.0369
3313	Electrometallurgical products	.0355
	First quartile	.0054
	Median	.0027
	Third quartile	.0016

Notes

Chapter 2

1. See Ohta (1974).
2. An example of the use of translog cost functions is given in Berndt and Wood (1975).
3. Greene (1983) uses a modified translog cost function which allows for economies of scale.
4. Brown (1980) reviews some of the problems encountered in aggregating across inputs and outputs.
5. One way to aggregate across firms is to assume that the differences between them can be characterized by an efficiency parameter which is distributed in some known way across firms. Houthakker (1955–56) introduced this concept, and it was later extended by Sato (1975).
6. Grunfeld and Griliches (1960) show that aggregation can improve the explanatory power of regression analysis when the model of individual behavior is not perfectly specified, and give some empirical examples. Ichniowski (1984) also finds evidence for these benefits of aggregation.
7. Miller (1983) points out a problem with the assumption of a constant depreciation rate over time, since firms are more likely to invest in new capital when rapid obsolescence is occurring.
8. Gordon (1983) notes that capital quality improvements may take the form of lower operating cost, also not captured in the capital price deflator.
9. For example, Berndt and Wood (1983) develop a procedure to adjust capital of different vintages for differences in energy efficiency. Also, Gordon (1983) finds that adjusting aircraft prices for declining operating costs yields falling prices during the 1957 to 1971 period, rather than the rising prices normally measured.

Chapter 3

1. Throughout this discussion we consider only pollution by firms. This is not because households produce no pollution, but because the empirical analysis presented later deals only with the regulation of firms.
2. This only holds if all polluters remain in production. In the longer run, polluters would face higher costs when they are forced to pay for their pollution, and would either shut down or raise prices, which would tend to reduce output and further reduce pollution.

Notes for Chapter 3

3. Each user would recognize that his own contribution paid for only a tiny part of the total cleanup. Therefore, few individuals would choose to contribute and little cleanup would be paid for.

4. Similar concerns with asymmetric information arise in the regulation of monopolies. Solutions to the problem have been found (see Loeb and Magat [1979] and Vogelsang and Finsinger [1979]), but these commonly require a "bribe" to the monopolist or assume naive behavior by firms over time. In general, Baron and Myerson (1982) show that the regulator cannot simultaneously achieve both efficiency and distributional goals.

5. Weitzman (1974) shows that quantity-based regulation is generally better if and only if the total benefits curve has more curvature near the optimum than the total cost curve. Roberts and Spence (1976) suggest a combination of licenses and effluent charges and subsidies to avoid the most serious cases of nonoptimality.

6. Of course they would prefer to have the monitoring overstate the extent of their cleanup, so there needs to be some verification procedure.

7. If polluting firms raise their prices to cover costs imposed by regulation, there may also be distributional consequences for consumers.

8. This is not to say that some cases of vigorous enforcement do not exist. However, these cases use large amounts of agency resources, and relatively few polluters in violation of the standards are taken to court.

9. The EPA has made some moves recently towards more efficient regulations, including mechanisms to allow a limited "trading" in emissions between plants. Crandall (1983) discusses such programs, which have seen only limited use so far.

10. For a more detailed discussion of employment hazards and market performance, see Viscusi (1979a).

11. This ignores issues of heterogeneity of worker preferences. Workers who care less about hazards would work in more risky jobs at a lower differential than the average worker would demand. Case (b) in figure 3.3 shows a case where only a few workers are needed for job B and workers' preferences are varied enough that W_B is lower than W_A.

12. It may be that workers in hazardous jobs systematically undervalue the risks of their employment, to reduce their own anxiety about the hazards (see Akerlof and Dickens [1982]). Also, Tversky and Kahneman (1974) present evidence that people do not use available information rationally when making decisions under uncertainty. However, Viscusi and O'Connor (1984) find that chemical workers do respond to information presented in chemical labels in evaluating the hazards of their job.

13. On the other hand, Dickens (1984) sees only limited evidence for the existence of compensating differentials, and finds a negative differential for the risk of fatal hazards among nonunion workers.

14. This assumes that workers should be permitted to 'trade' workplace protection for higher wages. If one believes that no workers should be exposed to excessive hazards, despite their apparent willingness to be so exposed, regulation of hazards might be necessary.

15. For example, one standard prohibited ice in drinking water.

16. This was the 1978 Barlow decision by the Supreme Court. This tactic has been used relatively infrequently, possibly because employers are concerned that an irritated inspector, returning with a search warrant, would be much more likely to find and cite violations.
17. As shown in Jones (1982) for asbestos regulation.

Chapter 4

1. We might be at a corner solution, given the zero price previously, so that there would be no reduction in pollution for some small nonzero pollution charge.
2. Viscusi (1983) shows that uncertainty, combined with irreversible investments, is likely to reduce investments. Alternatively, Myers and Nakamura (1980) note that regulatory constraints might speed up the obsolescence of existing capital, inducing greater investment in new capital. It is not clear which effect will predominate.
3. Although these delays are best known for power plants, Quarles (1979) notes that large industrial projects are also affected, with two or three year waits for permit approval (which is not always guaranteed).
4. On the other hand, old plants may be more seriously affected by regulation than new ones, if the regulator insists on applying the same standards to both. In this case there could be expanded opportunities for productive investment as the old plants shut down.
5. Ashford and Heaton (1983) and Hoerger et al. (1983) examine these impacts for the chemical industry. The latter study finds substantial costs of regulation, in terms of less R&D going to productive purposes and fewer new products developed.
6. Clark (1980) finds a similar positive shock effect for unionization of cement plants.
7. Alternatively, the new managers might be better at dealing with regulators but less capable at dealing with production matters, thereby lowering productivity.

Chapter 5

1. The description of the unexplained productivity growth as advances in technology is reinforced by studies such as Sveikauskas (1981) and Griliches (1980) which find measures of research and development activities exerting a significant, positive impact on productivity through 1969.
2. A recent study by Denison (1983) considers data from 1948 to 1981 and concludes that total factor productivity growth continued slow through 1981. Labor productivity growth since 1980 has shown substantial growth, as pointed out by Baily (1984). However, Clark (1984), using data through 1983, concludes that the recent productivity growth increase can be attributed to the cyclical recovery, rather than to a rebound in long-run productivity growth.
3. Some researchers find an earlier decline, beginning in 1965 or 1969. See for example, Nadiri and Schankerman (1981) or Norsworthy, Harper and Kunze (1979).
4. In fact, a similar decline in productivity growth was observed across all the developed Western economies at roughly the same time. This is documented in Lindbeck (1983) and Giersch and Wolter (1983). This research does not address the international aspects of the slowdown, concentrating solely on the U.S. experience.

Not everyone agrees that the slowdown has been as remarkable as the foregoing review suggests. Darby (1984) argues that controlling for labor force quality changes explains much of the slowdown, and that the rest is explained by the imposition and removal of price controls in the early 1970s.

5. The interested reader is referred to Denison (1979) for seventeen such proposed explanations.

Chapter 6

1. The Census Bureau's industry and product classifications are based on a system of increasing detail, with more detailed industries having more digits. Thus the 4-digit industry 2514, Metal Household Furniture, is located within the 3-digit industry 251, Household Furniture, which is itself part of the 2-digit industry 25, Furniture and Fixtures. The product classification scheme is more detailed, including up to 7-digit detail.
2. The author is grateful to Zvi Griliches and Frank Lichtenberg for making available their copy of the PCS data.
3. Based on 1977 Census of Manufacturing data for 423 industries.
4. Based on 1977 Census of Manufacturing data for 426 industries.
5. A list of these changes is available from the author.
6. This sector (Apparel and Other Textile Products) has a very large number of establishments which typically have very small pollution abatement expenditures. The Census Bureau omits the sector from the sample in order to concentrate observations on the remaining sectors which provide much more information on total compliance costs.
7. For example, in 1978, 67 4-digit industries had capital data present and 127 had operating cost data present. However, they represented 76 percent of capital and 89 percent of operating cost compliance expenditures.
8. Out of 29,216 manufacturing records, 910 were allocated to various 4-digit SIC codes and 1,076 could not be matched to any valid 4-digit SIC code.
9. Scherer actually develops two measures of R&D used, depending on whether R&D is treated as a public good ($1 of R&D done that benefits several industries counts as $1 for each industry) or a private good ($1 of R&D done that benefits several industries is allocated among the industries, a fraction each). The private good assumption is used here.

Chapter 7

1. The formula used is that presented in equation 2.12.
2. The results are not materially affected by extending the later time period to 1980 or changing the earlier period, though they are somewhat sensitive to the choice of 1973 as the starting year.
3. The regulation measures refer to a level of regulation during a year, while the productivity measures refer to productivity growth from one year to the next (measured at the end of the year). Therefore, productivity growth between 1973 and 1974 would be explained by 1974 regulation. Similarly, the five years of productivity growth from 1973 to 1978 are explained by five years of regulation data, 1974 to 1978.

4. The results obtained from an analysis of labor productivity growth are similar to those reported here for total factor productivity growth. Only total factor productivity results are reported here, because controlling for the usage of all inputs is needed to compare the productivity growth of different industries.
5. Section 7.5.3 examines the connection between input and output growth rates in greater detail.
6. Recall from chapter 5 Denison's (1979) estimates that pollution abatement and protection of employee safety and health explained 0.35 percent per year of the productivity slowdown. He concluded that regulation explained only 15 percent of the slowdown, partly because of his lower estimate of regulation's impact, but also because the slowdown for the private business sector (2.4 percent) greatly exceeded that for manufacturing.
7. See section 6.3.2 for an explanation of why the textile values are zero and how missing values were allocated.
8. Appendix table A.1 presents a list of the top 10 industries for each of the major regulation variables and some measures of the distribution of each variable.
9. This result might be expected if the constraints on firms' behavior imposed by regulation are especially costly in industries which are experiencing rapid changes in production techniques.
10. In section 6.3.2 we mentioned that operating cost is disaggregated by input type in the questionnaire. Unfortunately, these data are complete for only a few industries, and attempts to use the detailed data were unsuccessful.
11. As mentioned in footnote 6 above, the basic results suggest an impact of OSHA and EPA regulation on productivity somewhat larger than that calculated by Denison, who considered only the mismeasured input effect.

Chapter 8

1. The fractions used here are the fractions of all compliance expenditures accounted for by manufacturing, based on data from the U.S. Council on Environmental Quality report (1980) which presents estimates of total compliance costs, and the manufacturing cost data.
2. From U.S. Bureau of Labor Statistics (1980), which indicates that manufacturing was responsible for about 44 percent of all workplace injuries and 25 percent of fatalities.
3. One could argue that these abatement expenditures are a beneficial result of the EPA inspections, not a determinant of them. However, differences in changes in these expenditures over time are negatively (not positively) related to differences in the EPA inspection rates.

Bibliography

Akerlof, George A., and William T. Dickens, "The Economic Consequences of Cognitive Dissonance," *American Economic Review*, vol. 72, no. 3, 1982, pp. 307–19.

Ashford, Nicholas A., *Crisis in the Workplace: Occupational Disease and Injury*, Cambridge, Mass.: The MIT Press, 1976.

———, and George R. Heaton, Jr., "Regulation and Technological Innovation in the Chemical Industry," *Law and Contemporary Problems*, vol. 46, no. 3, Summer 1983, pp. 109–57.

Baily, Martin Neil, "The Productivity Growth Slowdown by Industry," *Brookings Papers on Economic Activity*, 1982(2), pp. 423–59.

———, "Will Productivity Growth Recover? Has It Done So Already?" *American Economic Review*, vol. 74, no. 2, 1984, pp. 231–35.

Baron, D., and R. Myerson, "Regulating a Monopolist with Unknown Costs," *Econometrica*, vol. 50, no. 4, 1982, pp. 911–30.

Bartel, Ann P., and Lacy Glenn Thomas, "OSHA Enforcement, Industrial Compliance and Workplace Injuries," Working Paper No. 953, Cambridge, Mass.: National Bureau of Economic Research, August 1982.

Berndt, Ernst R., and Mohammed S. Khaled, "Parametric Productivity Measurement and Choice Among Flexible Functional Forms," *Journal of Political Economy*, vol. 87, no. 6, 1979, pp. 1220–45.

Berndt, Ernst R., and David O. Wood, "Technology, Prices, and the Derived Demand for Energy," Review of Economics and Statistics, vol. 57, no. 3, 1975, pp. 259–68.

———, and David O. Wood, "Energy Price Changes and the Induced Revaluation of Durable Capital in U.S. Manufacturing," presented at NBER Summer Workshop on Investment and Productivity, July 1983.

Brown, Murray, "The Measurement of Capital Aggregates: A Postreswitching Problem," in *The Measurement of Capital*, Dan Usher, ed., Chicago: National Bureau of Economic Research, 1980.

Bruno, Michael, "Raw Materials, Profits and the Productivity Slowdown," *Quarterly Journal of Economics*, vol. 99, no. 1, February 1984, pp. 1–29.

Burrows, Paul, *The Economic Theory of Pollution Control*, Cambridge, Mass.: The MIT Press, 1980.

Christainsen, Gregory B., and Robert H. Haveman, "Public Regulations and the Slowdown in Productivity Growth," *American Economic Review*, vol. 71, no. 2, 1981, pp. 320–25.

Clark, Kim B., "The Impact of Unionization on Productivity: A Case Study," *Industrial and Labor Relations Review*, vol. 33, no. 4, 1980, pp. 451–69.

Clark, Peter K., "Productivity and Profits in the 1980s: Are They Really Improving?" *Brookings Papers on Economic Activity*, 1984 (1), pp. 133–67.

Cooke, William N., and Frederick H. Gautschi III, "OSHA, Plant Safety Programs and Injury Reduction," *Industrial Relations*, vol. 20, no. 3, 1981, pp. 245–57.

Crandall, Robert W., "Pollution Controls and Productivity Growth in Basic Industries," in *Productivity Measurement in Regulated Industries*, Thomas G. Cowing and Rodney E. Stevenson, eds., New York: Academic Press, 1981.

———, *Controlling Industrial Pollution: The Economics and Politics of Clean Air*, Washington: The Brookings Institution, 1983.

Darby, Michael R., "The U.S. Productivity Slowdown: A Case of Statistical Myopia," *American Economic Review*, vol. 74, no. 3, June 1984, pp. 301–22.

Denison, Edward F., "Final Comments," in *The Measurement of Productivity*, Washington: The Brookings Institution, 1972.

———, *Accounting for United States Economic Growth, 1929–69*, Washington: The Brookings Institution, 1974.

———, *Accounting for Slower Economic Growth: The United States in the 1970s*, Washington: The Brookings Institution, 1979.

———, "The Interruption of Productivity Growth in the United States," *The Economic Journal*, vol. 93, no. 369, 1983, pp. 56–77.

Dickens, William T., "Differences Between Risk Premiums in Union and Non-Union Wages and the Case for Occupational Safety Regulation," *American Economic Review*, vol. 74, no. 2, May 1984, pp. 320–23.

Fraumeni, Barbara M., and Dale W. Jorgenson, "Capital Formation and U.S. Productivity Growth, 1948–76," in *Productivity Analysis: A Range of Perspectives*, Ali Dogramaci, ed., Boston: Martinus Nijhoff Publishing, 1981.

Freeman, A. Myrick, "The Benefits of Air and Water Pollution Control: A Review and Synthesis of Recent Efforts," report prepared for U.S. Council on Environmental Quality, December 1979.

Giersch, Herbert, and Frank Wolter, "Towards an Explanation of the Productivity Slowdown: An Acceleration-Deceleration Hypothesis," *The Economic Journal*, vol. 93, no. 369, 1983, pp. 35–55.

Gollop, Frank M., and Mark J. Roberts, "Environmental Regulations and Productivity Growth: The Case of Fossil-fueled Electric Power Generation," *Journal of Political Economy*, vol. 91, no. 4, 1983, pp. 654–74.

Gordon, Robert J., "Energy Efficiency, User-Cost Change, and the Measurement of Durable Goods Prices," in *The U.S. National Income and Product Accounts: Selected Topics*, Murray F. Foss, ed., Chicago: University of Chicago Press, 1983.

Green, Mark, and Norman Waitzman, "Business War on the Law: An Analysis of the Benefits of Federal Health/Safety Enforcement," Washington: The Corporate Accountability Research Group, 1979.

Greene, W. H., "Simultaneous Estimation of Factor Substitution, Economies of Scale, Productivity, and Non-Neutral Technical Change," in *Developments in Econometric Analyses of Productivity: Measurement and Modeling Issues*, Ali Dogramaci, ed., Boston: Kluwer-Nijhoff Publishing, 1983.

Griliches, Zvi, "R&D and the Productivity Slowdown," *American Economic Review*, vol. 70, no. 2, 1980, pp. 343–48.

———, and Dale W. Jorgenson, "Issues in Growth Accounting: A Reply to Edward F. Denison," *Survey of Current Business*, vol. 52, no. 5, Part II, 1972, pp. 65–94.

———, and Frank Lichtenberg, "R+D and Productivity Growth at the Industry Level: Is There Still a Relationship?," in *R+D, Patents and Productivity*, Zvi Griliches, ed., Chicago: University of Chicago Press, 1984.

Grunfeld, Yehuda, and Zvi Griliches, "Is Aggregation Necessarily Bad?" *Review of Economics and Statistics*, vol. 62, no. 1, 1960, pp. 1–13.

Haveman, Robert H., and Gregory B. Christainsen, "Environmental Regulations and Productivity Growth," in *Environmental Regulation and the U.S. Economy*, Henry M. Peskin, Paul R. Portney and Allen V. Kneese, eds., Baltimore: Johns Hopkins University Press, 1981.

Herbert, J. H., "A Policy Model of Industrial Accidents Using Economics and Business Activity Variables," *Applied Economics*, vol. 11, June 1979, pp. 211-20.

Hoerger, Fred, William H. Beamer, and James S. Hanson, "The Cumulative Impact of Health, Environmental, and Safety Concerns on the Chemical Industry During the Seventies," *Law and Contemporary Problems*, vol. 46, no. 3, Summer 1983, pp. 59-107.

Houthakker, Hendrik S., "The Pareto Distribution and the Cobb-Douglas Production Function in Activity Analysis," *Review of Economic Studies*, vol. 23, no. 1, 1955-56, pp. 27-31.

Ichniowski, Casey, "Micro-Production Functions Aren't Pretty: Firm-Level and Industry-Level Specification for Inputs and Outputs," May 1984.

Jones, Carol Adaire, "Models of Regulatory Enforcement and Compliance," presented at the Winter Meetings of the Econometric Society, December 1982.

Jorgenson, Dale W., "Energy Prices and Productivity Growth," *Scandinavian Journal of Economics*, vol. 83, no. 2, 1981, pp. 165-79.

Kappler, Fredrick G., and Gary L. Rutledge, "Stock of Plant and Equipment for Air and Water Pollution Abatement in the United States, 1960-1981," *Survey of Current Business*, vol. 62, no. 11, 1982, pp. 18-25.

Kendrick, John W., *Postwar Productivity Trends in the United States*, New York: National Bureau of Economic Research, 1973.

_____, *Interindustry Differences in Productivity Growth*, Washington: American Enterprise Institute, 1983.

_____, and Elliot S. Grossman, *Productivity in the United States: Trends and Cycles*, Baltimore: Johns Hopkins University Press, 1980.

Kopp, Raymond J., and V. Kerry Smith, "Productivity Measurement and Environmental Regulation: An Engineering-Econometric Analysis," in *Productivity Measurement in Regulated Industries*, Thomas G. Cowing and Rodney Stevenson, eds., New York: Academic Press, 1981.

Lave, Lester B., and Seskin, Eugene P., *Air Pollution and Human Health*, Baltimore: Johns Hopkins University Press, 1977.

Leibenstein, Harvey, "Allocative Efficiency vs. 'X-Efficiency'," *American Economic Review*, vol. 56, no. 3, 1966, pp. 392-415.

Lindbeck, Assar, "The Recent Slowdown of Productivity Growth," *The Economic Journal*, vol. 93, no. 369, 1983, pp. 13-34.

Loeb, M., and W. A. Magat, "A Decentralized Model of Utility Regulation," *Journal of Law and Economics*, vol. 22, 1979, pp. 399-404.

Marlow, Michael L., "The Economics of Enforcement (the Case of OSHA)," *Journal of Economics and Business*, vol. 34, no. 2, 1982, pp. 165-71.

McCaffrey, David P., "An Assessment of OSHA's Recent Effects on Injury Rates," *Journal of Human Resources*, vol. 18, no. 1, 1983, pp. 131-46.

Mendeloff, John, *Regulating Safety: An Econometric and Political Analysis of Occupational Safety and Health Policy*, Cambridge, Mass.: MIT Press, 1979.

Mendelsohn, Robert and Guy Orcutt, "An Empirical Analysis of Air Pollution Dose-Response Curves," *Journal of Environmental Economics and Management*, vol. 6, June 1979, pp. 85-106.

Miller, E. M., "A Difficulty in Measuring Productivity with a Perpetual Inventory Capital Stock Measure," *Oxford Bulletin of Economics and Statistics*, vol. 45, no. 3, August 1983, pp. 297-306.

Myers, John G., and Leonard Nakamura, "Energy and Pollution Effects on Productivity: A Putty-Clay Approach," in *New Developments in Productivity Measurement and Analysis,* John W. Kendrick and Beatrice N. Vaccara, eds., Chicago: The University of Chicago Press, 1980.

Nadiri, M. Ishaq, "Sectoral Productivity Slowdown," *American Economic Review,* vol. 70, no. 2, 1980, pp. 349–52.

———, and M. A. Schankerman, "Technical Change, Returns to Scale and the Productivity Slowdown," *American Economic Review,* vol. 71, no. 2, 1981, pp. 314–19.

Nichols, Albert J., *Targeting Economic Incentives for Environmental Protection,* Cambridge, Mass.: The MIT Press, 1984.

Norsworthy, J. R., Michael J. Harper, and Kent Kunze, "The Slowdown in Productivity Growth: Analysis of Some Contributing Factors," *Brookings Papers on Economic Activity,* 1979(2), pp. 387–421.

Ohta, M., "A Note on the Duality between Production and Cost Functions: Rate of Return to Scale and Rate of Technical Progress," *Economic Studies Quarterly,* vol. 25, December 1974, pp. 63–65.

Pashigian, B. Peter, "The Effect of Environmental Regulation on Optimal Plant Size and Factor Shares," *Journal of Law and Economics,* vol. 27, no. 1, April 1984, pp. 1–28.

Portney, Paul R., "The Macroeconomic Impacts of Federal Environmental Regulation," in *Environmental Regulation and the U.S. Economy,* Henry M. Peskin, Paul R. Portney, and Allen V. Kneese, eds., Baltimore: Johns Hopkins University Press, 1981.

Quarles, John, "Federal Regulation of New Industrial Plants," Monograph No. 28, *BNA Environmental Reporter,* vol. 10, no. 1, May 4, 1979.

Roberts, Marc J., and Michael Spence, "Effluent Charges and Licenses Under Uncertainty," *Journal of Public Economics,* vol. 5, no. 3-4, 1976, pp. 193–208.

Ruff, Larry E., "Federal Environmental Regulation," in *The Study on Federal Regulation of the Senate Committee on Governmental Affairs* vol. 6, Washington: U.S. Government Printing Office, December 1978.

Sato, Kazuo, *Production Functions and Aggregation,* Amsterdam: North-Holland Publishing Company, 1975.

Scherer, F. M., "Using Linked Patent and R&D Data to Measure Inter-Industry Technology Flows," presented at NBER Conference on R&D, Patents, and Productivity, October 1981.

———, "Inter-industry Technology Flows and Productivity Growth," *Review of Economics and Statistics,* vol. 64, no. 4, 1982, pp. 627–34.

Siegal, Robin, "Why Has Productivity Slowed Down?" *Data Resources Review,* vol. 1, March 1979, pp. 1.59–1.65.

Smith, Robert Stewart, "The Impact of OSHA Inspections on Manufacturing Injury Rates," *Journal of Human Resources,* vol. 14, no. 2, 1979, pp. 145–70.

Sveikauskas, Leo, "Technological Inputs and Multivactor Productivity Growth," *Review of Economics and Statistics,* vol. 63, no. 2, 1981, pp. 275–82.

Thaler, R., and S. Rosen, "The Value of Saving a Life: Evidence from the Labor Market," in *Household Production and Consumption,* Nestor Terleckyj, ed., New York: Columbia University Press, 1976.

Tversky, A., and D. Kahneman, "Judgement Under Uncertainty: Heuristics and Biases," *Science,* vol. 185, 1974, pp. 1124–31.

U.S. Bureau of Labor Statistics, "Occupational Injuries and Illnesses in the United States by Industry, 1978," Bulletin 2078, Washington: U.S. Government Printing Office, August 1980.

———, "Trends in Multifactor Productivity, 1948–1981," Bulletin 2178, Washington: U.S. Government Printing Office, September 1983.

U.S. Council on Environmental Quality, *Environmental Quality,* eleventh annual report, Washington: U.S. Government Printing Office, 1980.

Viscusi, W. Kip, *Employment Hazards: An Investigation of Market Performance*, Cambridge, Mass.: Harvard University Press, 1979 (a).

———, "The Impact of Occupational Safety and Health Regulation," *Bell Journal of Economics*, vol. 10, no. 1, 1979 (b), pp. 117–40.

———, "Frameworks for Analyzing the Effects of Risk and Environmental Regulations on Productivity," *American Economic Review*, vol. 73, no. 4, September 1983, pp. 793–801.

———, and Charles J. O'Connor, "Adaptive Responses to Chemical Labelling: Are Workers Bayesian Decision-Makers?" *American Economic Review*, vol. 74, no. 5, December 1984, pp. 942–56.

Vogelsang, I., and J. Finsinger, "A Regulatory Adjustment Process for Optimal Pricing by Multiproduct Monopoly Firms," *Bell Journal of Economics*, vol. 10, no. 1, 1979, pp. 151–71.

Waddell, T. E., "The Economic Damages of Air Pollution," EPA Publication, Socioeconomic Environmental Series, 1974.

Weisskopf, Thomas E., Samuel Bowles, and David M. Gordon, "Hearts and Minds: A Social Model of U.S. Productivity Growth," *Brookings Papers on Economic Activity*, 1983 (2), pp. 381–450.

Weitzman, Martin L., "Prices vs. Quantities," *Review of Economic Studies*, vol. 61, no. 4, 1974, pp. 477–91.

Zeckhauser, Richard, and Albert Nichols, "The Occupational Safety and Health Administration: An Overview," in *The Study on Federal Regulation of the Senate Committee on Governmental Affairs*, vol. 6, Washington: U.S. Government Printing Office, December 1978.

Index

Aggregation, 103nn5,6
Air Quality Control Act (1967), 21
Annual Survey of Manufacturers (ASM), 55–56, 57–58, 60

BLS
    See Labor Statistics, Bureau of

Census, Bureau of, 55, 58, 106n1, 107n2
    Pollution Abatement Costs and Expenditures Survey, 60–61
Census of Manufactures (COM), 55, 56, 57–58
Clean Air Act (1970), 21–22

Data description, 55–60
    accident rate, industrial, 65
    asymmetric information, 104n3
    PCS project data, 55–58

Environmental issues, 14–16
    pre-EPA, 21–22
    regulatory solutions, *see* Environmental Protection Agency
    workplace issues vs., 25–26
Environmental Protection Agency (EPA), 13–14, 14–25, 83
    compliance costs, 60–61, 81
    Compliance Data Systems (CSD), 63
        problems with, 63
    concerns of, 16–20
    distributional consequences, 20, 104n7
    enforcement, 20, 23–24, 63–64, 104nn8,9, 107n3
    federal legislation, 21–22
    National Emissions Data Systems (NEDS), 66, 93
    regulatory solutions, 16–21
    optimal outcomes and market failures, 14–16
    standards, 22–23
    summary, 24–25, 35
    theoretical issues, summarized, 21
    See also Regulation

Federal Water Pollution Control Act Amendments (1972), 22

Growth accounting, 7–8, 82–87
    problems with, 8–11

Health, Education and Welfare, Department of, 31

Industrial Economics, Bureau of, 59
Industry's behavior, regulatory impact on, 37–38
    See also Productivity
Industry Priority Report (OSHA), 65–66

Labor, Department of, 31
Labor productivity, 68
    slowdown, evidence of, 45–47
Labor Statistics, Bureau of (BLS), 45, 59, 65
Legislation, federal
    environmental, 21–22
    occupational, 31

Management Information System (MIS) database (OSHA), 62–63, 64
McGraw-Hill survey on capital spending, 60

National Ambient Air Quality Standards, 22
National Emissions Data System (NEDS), 66, 93

116 Index

National Institute for Occupational Safety and Health (NIOSH), 31, 65
National Safety Council, 92

Occupational Safety and Health Act (1970), 31
Occupational Safety and Health Administration (OSHA), 29-30, 83
   benefits, potential, 25-28, 91-93, 93-96
   benefits, targeting of, 93
   compliance costs, 60, 81
   enforcement, 33-34, 62-63, 81
   federal legislation, 31
   Industry Priority Report, 65-66
   Management Information System (MIS)
      database, 62-63, 64
      problems with, 62
   optimal outcome, 25-28
   regulations, 13-14
   standards, 31-33
   summary, 34, 35
   See also Regulation
Occupational Safety and Health Review Commission (OSHRC), 31, 33

PCS Project, 55, 57-59
   Annual Surveys of Manufacturers (ASM), 55-56, 57-58, 60
   Census of Manfacturers (COM), 55, 56, 57-58
   focus of, 59
Pennsylvania, University of, 55
Pollution, 103nn1,2
   See also Environmental Protection Agency
Pollution Abatement Costs and Expenditures Survey, 60-61
Productivity, regulation's impact on, 37-44, 49-54
   constraints and adjustment costs, 39-40
   empirical analysis
      extensions and tests, 81-87
         growth accounting, 82-87
         other impacts, 82
         predicted results, 81-82
      objections to, 73-80
         capital stock, measured, 77
         macroeconomic performance, 77
         measurement
            problems, 73-74
            usage/intensity, 76-77
         outliers and non-linearity, 74-76
         research and development decline, 77-80
      panel data analysis, 87-88
   investments and, 40-41, 105n2
   measured, 38-39
   modeling, 42-44
   positive impacts, 42
   research and development, 41, 42
Productivity growth
   accounting, 7-8, 82-87
      problems with, 8-11
   decline in, 105n4
   measured of, 68
   unexplained, 105n1
Productivity measurement techniques
   estimation, 6-7
   methods, choice of, 6
   problems with, 8-11
      assumptions, 8-9
      implementation, 9-11
   single factor, 11
   total factor, 8-11
Productivity models, 3-5
   Cobb-Douglas, 3-4, 7
   general case approximation, 4-5
   second order approximation, 5, 6
Productivity: regulation relationship, 68-73, 88-90
Productivity slowdown, 45-54
   evidence of, 45-49
      labor, 45-47
      total factor, 47-49
   explanations, 49-52
   previous studies, 52-54
   summary, 54

Regulation
   benefits of, 91-96
   compliance costs, 60-62
   enforcement, 62-65
   productivity relationship, 67-73, 88-90
   quantity-based, 104n5
   See also Environmental Protection Agency; Occupational Safety and Health Administration
Regulation, impact of
   on firm's behavior, 37-38
   modeling, 42-44
   on productivity, 37-44, 49, 54
      empirical analysis of, 67-90

"Regulatory shock," 42
Research and development data, 41, 42, 65
  decline of, 51, 77-80

Spearman rank correlation measure, 75
SRI, Inc., 53
Standard Industrial Classification (SIC), 55
  problems with, 57, 58, 62, 63-64, 66
State Implementation Plan (SIP), 22

Total factor productivity studies, 8-11, 47-49, 67, 68

U.S. Council of Environmental Quality, 107n1

Water Quality Control Act (1965), 21
Workers compensation, 31
Worker's preference, 104n11
Workplace/worker safety, 25-35
  accident rate data, industrial, 65
  environmental issues vs., 25-26
  nonunion, 104n13
  pre-OSHA, 30-31
  regulatory solution, *See* Occupational Safety and Health Administration
  workers' health protection, 28